Harvest Poems

Carl Sandburg was born of Swedish immigrant parents in Galesburg, Illinois, in 1878. Unknown to the literary world until he was thirty-six, in 1914 he won a prize for a group of poems, including the now famous "Chicago." Two years later he published his first volume, *Chicago Poems*, which with five more volumes of his poetry—*Cornhuskers; Smoke and Steel; Slabs of the Sunburnt West; Good Morning, America; The People, Yes*—were gathered together in *Complete Poems*, awarded the Pulitzer Prize for Poetry in 1951. Sandburg is also the author of the children's classic *Rootabaga Stories;* a collection of folksongs, *The American Songbag;* a novel, *Remembrance Rock;* an autobiography, *Always the Young Strangers;* and a six-volume biography of Abraham Lincoln, the last four volumes of which (*Abraham Lincoln: The War Years*) received the Pulitzer Prize for History in 1940.

"More volubly than any poet since Whitman," Louis Untermeyer says in his *Lives of the Poets*, "Sandburg ranged over the United States. . . . [He] looks the roving troubadour—an ancient Viking who speaks and sings with a pronounced midwestern drawl. The drawl is in his writing, the slow, rambling transcriptions of the skald who made himself a national bard."

Carl Sandburg

Harvest Poems

1910–1960

With an Introduction by
Mark Van Doren

A Harvest/HBJ Book
Harcourt Brace Jovanovich, Publishers
San Diego   New York   London

INTRODUCTION BY MARK VAN DOREN

Carl Sandburg, like all of the other American poets who came into prominence with him, brought something back to poetry that had been sadly missing in the early years of this century. It was humor, the indispensable ingredient of art as it is of life. Just as we cannot take a man seriously who lacks the sense of humor, so we cannot take a poet. Humor is the final sign and seal of seriousness, for it is a proof that reality is held in honor and in love. The little poets whom the renaissance of more than forty years ago swept into oblivion were first of all unreal; their poems were not about anything that matters; and so their feelings—or the ones they said they had—failed to be impressive. They had no genuine subjects.

It is often said of the renaissance in question that the chief thing about it was its discovery of new styles. But this was secondary to the discovery of new subjects, or, rather, of old ones long neglected. Edwin Arlington Robinson restored wit to its empty throne, along with ideas and ironies which narrative helped him state. Edgar Lee Masters in the *Spoon River Anthology* went all the way back to Greece for the view he would take of men and women in a contemporary village. Vachel Lindsay romped through hells and heavens of his own devising, but he romped. Robert Frost spoke with a living voice of people who lived no less than he; and there was a wryness in this voice, an indirection and an understatement so convincing that his readers scarcely knew what moved them. Ezra Pound rediscovered society as a subject, first in minor ways and then in a way which at least for him was major. T. S. Eliot, witty always, did not rest until he had wrung paradoxes and puzzles out of theology. Wallace Stevens tried his hand at assessing the very form and content—if content—of the modern imagination. The list could be longer, but now here is Carl Sandburg, and what shall be said of the things he discovered?

Once more there are those who would say that the style in his case is the man: the free verse, the long, looping lines that run on like prose and yet are not prose, the commitment to the vernacular, or, as he likes to put it, the lingo of a people. Once more, however, I would say that the first thing with him is his view of the world, which, to be sure, his style frees him to express but which is, above all, there to be expressed. And what is this view? The question is not easy to answer, for his critic or for him. It is, to begin with, a broad view, even a huge one, that takes in everything visible and a good many further things that are invisible because they are all but too fine for words. Then there is the question of how he looks at this big scene, and of what goes on behind his eyes as he beholds it. The answer probably is that the sense of humor in him is more than anything else the sense of the absurd, or, as he might say, the cockeyed, the loony, the goofy. The scene before him is so crowded with anomalies and discrepancies that he scarcely knows what to think or say about it. He can be angry, of course, in a downright, forthright way; but he is just as likely to grin as gargoyles do, expecting neither amelioration nor excuse: the world is this way, so that is the way it is. And his style, granted, liberates him so that he may suggest all this; it gives him entry into steel mills and mean streets, into shacks along the railroad, into the hearts of obscure people to whom he feels allegiance, and of course also into the fresh winds and sweet odors that find their way into these places and then go innocently on to the farthest reaches of moon or star. The anomalies are gulfs which only a giant might hope to jump across; so Sandburg jumps, and as often as not lands safely on the other side. He can never make up his mind, however, upon one point. Does the world make a lot of sense or does it make no sense at all? His round trips back and forth between these extremes of conviction are what his poetry, as I see and hear it, consists of. And they are long trips, with many stopovers, nor does the man who takes them fail to feel at home anywhere. Thomas Carlyle once remarked that the presence of humor in a poet—he meant Shakespeare chiefly—enables him to see what is beneath him and about him as well as what is above him. The ideal poet, as Schiller had said, yearns only up and off. But the real poet studies the world as it is: lovely, terrible, sensible, grotesque; and would ask for no other one in its place. In this sense, Sandburg is a real poet, so that it is no wonder people trust him and adore him.

The shovelman who works ten hours a day

> Keeping the road-bed so the roses and jonquils
> Shake hardly at all in the cut glass vases
> Standing slender on the tables in the dining cars

—there is Sandburg's humor, feeding on a contrast so gross that you would think the passengers at the tables were bound to see it too; but they don't, because the flowers "shake hardly at all"—the telling phrase, the barely stated fact which, nevertheless, a whole poem is built upon. The strange phenomenon of fingerprints, or thumb prints as Sandburg has it, namely that no two of them are alike, is more than strange to this poet; it is a mystery of such proportions that he assumes "a Great God of Thumbs who can tell the inside story of this." Is a Hallowe'en pumpkin fearful or funny? Children understand:

> I am a jack-o'-lantern
> With terrible teeth
> And the children know
> I am fooling.

Then what about "the horses looking over a fence in the frost of late October saying good morning to the horses hauling wagons of rutabaga to market"? It is hard to define the humor in that; it calls so little attention to itself, but it lurks in every word, and is silent as horse laughter truly is. "A high majestic fooling" is omnipresent in these pages, whether wind and corn are talking things over together, or the milkman "puts a bottle on six hundred porches and calls it a day's work," or the children of the hangman when he is home in the evening "stay off some topics," or the "people of the eaves," the wrens, have as much trouble keeping house as husbands and wives do. "People of the eaves, I wish you good morning, I wish you a thousand thanks," says the poet to the birds. "The little two-legged joker, Man" is in perspective no more momentous than the wren. Both creatures magnify their own importance, identifying themselves with their Maker:

> There are men and women so lonely they believe
> God, too, is lonely.

Yet now and then there is a man who knows so well what he wants that he does not care who laughs at him, even Sandburg. Such is the man who was "foolish about windows," and I guess it was Sandburg himself. Anyhow, as he had a carpenter put more and bigger windows in his house

> One neighbor said, "If you keep on you'll be
>   able to see everything there is."
> I answered, "That'll be all right, that'll be
>   classy enough for me."
> Another neighbor said, "Pretty soon your house
>   will be all windows."
> And I said, "Who would the joke be on then?"

But the biggest joke is death: so serious a matter really that Sandburg must take refuge in a gargoyle grin that makes no pretense of understanding the plainest of all things to see—and yet few see it. Certainly not the man on the train in "Limited":

> I am riding on a limited express, one of the crack
>   trains of the nation.
> Hurtling across the prairie into blue haze and dark air

> go fifteen all-steel coaches holding a thousand
> people.
> (All the coaches shall be scrap and rust and all the
> men and women laughing in the diners and
> sleepers shall pass to ashes.)
> I ask a man in the smoker where he is going and he
> answers: "Omaha."

Walt Whitman, to whom Sandburg is supposed to owe an almost unpayable debt, but to whom he cannot owe his humor because Whitman had none to lend, was of the opinion that America needed "great poems of death," and indeed he wrote the two greatest that we have in "Out of the Cradle" and "When Lilacs Last." But Whitman could not have written "Limited," great as he was, or, for that matter, "Cool Tombs"; and certainly not "Grass," which is justly one of Sandburg's most famous poems.

> Shovel them under and let me work.
> Two years, ten years, and passengers ask the conductor:
> What place is this?
> Where are we now?
>
>
> I am the grass.
> Let me work.

"All I can give you," says this poet, "is broken-face gargoyles." It is for him to speak of Death as one who "comes with a master-key and lets himself in and says: We'll go now." Death is an iron door that shuts out all sound, so that he can say:

> Be silent about it; since at the gates of tombs
> silence is a gift, be silent; since at the epitaphs
> written in the air, since at the swan songs hung in
> the air, silence is a gift, be silent; forget it.

Yet he can never forget it either. It is his central subject, the very stuff of his art: "Poetry is the harnessing of the paradox of earth cradling life and then entombing it." Death is as vast and ancient as the Sphinx, but then again it comes on little cat feet, like the fog. It is a pitiless skull, but then again it is "a beautiful friend who remembers." It is anything and everything. Remember it, forget it.

"What place is this? Where are we now?" This could be Sandburg's motto, but also it is a reminder of the parallelism that regularly marks his style. He owes more here to the Bible than he does to Whitman.

They tell me you are wicked and I believe them. . . .

And they tell me you are crooked and I answer. . . .

And they tell me you are brutal and my reply is. . . .

There on his opening page is a conspicuous example; and farther on, in the poem "Chicago," is an equally Job-like line:

> Laughing even as an ignorant fighter laughs who
> has never lost a battle.

This modern poet is venerable, too, just as this boisterous one can speak softly when he pleases: the gargoyle covers a face that is friendly to the finest feelings. Thomas Hardy said in one of his poems that he hoped after his death to be spoken of as a man who had "noticed" things. To notice is more than anything else to be a poet and a man. Sandburg continually touches us by his power to be aware of fugitive circumstances that betray deep truth. There was the family in "Clean Curtains," for instance, that moved to the corner of Congress and Green Streets and tried for a while to keep their windows "the same as the rim of a nun's bonnet"; but dust won out and the curtains disappeared. There was the red-headed restaurant cashier whom he wrote a poem to assure that

> Around and around go ten thousand men hunting a red-headed
> girl with two freckles on her chin.

And of course there were the people of the eaves: "The house of a wren will not run itself any more than the house of a man." There was also the wind in the orchard that taught him how to sleep, "counting its money and throwing it away." There was the telephone wire, with death and laughter passing through it and yet it had to admit:

> Slim against the sun I make not even a clear line of
> shadow.

Nor let us forget a certain invisible goddess:

> The woman named Tomorrow
> sits with a hairpin in her teeth
> and takes her time
> and does her hair the way she wants it
> and fastens at last the last braid and coil
> and puts the hairpin where it belongs
> and turns and drawls: Well, what of it?
> My grandmother, Yesterday, is gone.
> What of it? Let the dead be dead.

From NOTES FOR A PREFACE

The inexplicable is all around us. So is the incomprehensible. So is the unintelligible. Interviewing Babe Ruth in 1928, I put it to him, "People come and ask what's your system for hitting home runs— that so?" "Yes," said the Babe, "and all I can tell 'em is I pick a good one and sock it. I get back to the dugout and they ask me what it was I hit and I tell 'em I don't know except it looked good."

All around us the imponderable and the unfathomed—at these targets many a poet has shot his bullets of silver and scored a bull's-eye, or missed with dull pellets of paper.

Will Rogers, twirling his cowhand rope, insisted, "We are all ignorant but on different subjects." And in Chicago we heard William Butler Yeats quote his father, "What can be explained is not poetry."

The Spanish poet Lorca saw one plain apple infinite as the sea. "The life of an apple when it is a delicate flower to the moment when, golden russet, it drops from the tree into the grass is as mysterious and as great as the perpetual rhythm of the tides. And a poet must know this."

There are poets of the cloister and the quiet corner, of green fields and the earth serene in its changes. There are poets of streets and struggles, of dust and combat, of violence wanton or justified, of plain folk living close to a hard earth as in the great though neglected poem *Piers Plowman*. There have been poets whose themes wove through both of the foregoing approaches.

Poetry and politics, the relation of the poets to society, to democracy, to monarchy, to dictatorships—we have here a theme whose classic is yet to be written.

A poet explains for us what for him is poetry by what he presents to us in his poems. A painter makes definitions of what for him is art by the kind of paintings his brush puts on canvas. An actor defines dramatic art as best he can by the way he plays his parts. The playwright in his offering of dramatic action and lines tells us what he regards as theater art. The novelist explains his theory of creative literature by the stories and people in his books. And so on down the line. There is no escape. There stands the work of the man, the woman who wrought it. We go to it, read it, look at it, perhaps go back to it many a time and it is for each of us what we make of it. The creator of it can say it means this or that—or it means for you whatever you take it to mean. He can say it happened, it came into being and it now exists apart from him and nothing can be done about it.

No two persons register precisely the same to a work of art. Mark Twain tells, as one version has it, of two men who for the first time laid eyes on the tumultuous and majestic Grand Canyon of Arizona. One cried out, "I'll be God damned!" The other fell to his knees in prayer. Mark contended their religious feelings were the same though the ritual was different.

After the first performance of Strauss's *Salome* in Berlin, the *Tageblatt*'s music critic raved against it. Seeing Grieg in the lobby he asked the Norwegian composer, "What do you think of it?" The reply came cool as a cube of iced cucumber, "How can I tell you that? I have heard it only once."

Of Turner's painting *The Slave Ship*, Ruskin wrote it was "perfect and immortal." The painter Inness declared, "It's claptrap." Thackeray was puzzled and neutral: "I don't know whether it's sublime or ridiculous."

As years pass and experience writes new records in our mind life, we go back to some works of art we rejected in the early days and find values we missed. Work, love, laughter, pain, death, put impressions on us as time passes, and we brood over what has happened, praying it may be an "exalted brooding." Out of songs and scars and the mystery of personal development, we may get eyes that pick out intentions we had not seen before in people, in art, in books and poetry.

Naturally, too, the reverse happens. What we register to at one period of life, what we find gay and full of fine nourishment at one time, we may find later has lost interest for us. A few masterpieces last across the years. We usually discard some. A few masterpieces are enough. Why this is so we do not know. For each individual his new acquisitions and old discards are different.

Perhaps no wrong is done and no temple of human justice violated in pointing out that each authentic poet makes a style of his own. Sometimes this style is so clearly the poet's own that when he is imitated it is known who is imitated. Shakespeare, Villon, Li Po, Whitman—each sent forth his language and impress of thought and feeling from a different style of gargoyle spout. In the spacious highways of books major or minor, each poet is allowed the stride that will get him where he wants to go if, God help him, he can hit that stride and keep it.

At the age of six, as my fingers first found how to shape the alphabet, I decided to become a person of letters. At the age of ten

I had scrawled letters on slates, on paper, on boxes and walls and I formed an ambition to become a sign-painter. At twenty I was an American soldier in Puerto Rico writing letters printed in the home town paper. At twenty-one I went to West Point, being a classmate of Douglas MacArthur and Ulysses S. Grant III—for two weeks—returning home after passing in spelling, geography, history, failing in arithmetic and grammar. At twenty-three I edited a college paper and wrote many a paragraph that after a lapse of fifty years still seems funny, the same applying to the college yearbook I edited the following year. Across several years I wrote many odd pieces—two slim books—not worth later reprint. In a six-year period came four books of poetry having a variety of faults, no other person more keenly aware of their accomplishments and shortcomings than myself. In the two books for children, in this period, are a few cornland tales that go on traveling, one about "The Two Skyscrapers Who Decided to Have a Child." At fifty I had published a two-volume biography and *The American Songbag,* and there was puzzlement as to whether I was a poet, a biographer, a wandering troubadour with a guitar, a midwest Hans Christian Andersen, or a historian of current events whose newspaper reporting was gathered into a book, *The Chicago Race Riots.* At fifty-one I wrote America's first biography of a photographer. At sixty-one came a four-volume biography, bringing doctoral degrees at Harvard, Yale, New York University, Wesleyan, Lafayette, Lincoln Memorial, Syracuse, Rollins, Dartmouth—Augustana and Uppsala at Stockholm. I am still studying verbs and the mystery of how they connect nouns. I am more suspicious of adjectives than at any other time in all my born days. I have forgotten the meaning of twenty or thirty of my poems written thirty or forty years ago. I still favor several simple poems published long ago which continue to have an appeal for simple people. I have written by different methods and in a wide miscellany of moods and have seldom been afraid to travel in lands and seas where I met fresh scenes and new songs. All my life I have been trying to learn to read, to see and hear, and to write. At sixty-five I began my first novel, and the five years lacking a month I took to finish it, I was still traveling, still a seeker. I should like to think that as I go on writing there will be sentences truly alive, with verbs quivering, with nouns giving color and echoes. It could be, in the grace of God, I shall live to be eighty-nine, as did Hokusai, and speaking my farewell to earthly scenes, I might paraphrase: "If God had let me live five years longer I should have been a writer."

Carl Sandburg
(in *Complete Poems,* 1950)

CONTENTS

Cornhuskers

Smoke and Steel

Slabs of the Sunburnt West

Complete Poems   ·

The Sandburg Range

New Poems

Poetry is dead? So they say.
Yes, ya betcha, ja ja, oui oui, si si.
quite so,   indeed,   to be sure,
correct, right on the nose, the button.
And the next bus is a long wait,
don't run any more, been taken off.

Aye aye, poetry is done for, vanished, kicked the bucket
and gone up the flue and lost in the mountain snows of
the latest plane crash, hunting parties on the way to
gather the remains and study the debris.

Okay and let 'er go, in every time and age someone must
stand up and say it again: "Ah me, tut tut, alas and
alack, woe is us or maybe it's just as well, poetry is
on a slab in the morgue, nameless, unidentified, two
blue holes in her back from an ice pick, a clean job,
one more ice pick murder, as sweet a gal as Lehigh Valley
Nell, done in by her own pals and that's no malarky,
gangway now, give her the gate to a free public grave-
yard"—this though the coroner, the jurors, six men good
and true, must yet sift every scintilla of evidence
bearing on the two blue holes and who drove the ice pick.

Or she could be a cadaver we have seen certified as
dead from anemia and lack of love and they conducted
a ritual service in a mortuary establishment dedicated
to the dignity of death and the rakeoff on the coffin
they carry you off in: one grand, a thousand smackers
of the coin of the realm, for a casket of copper lined
with mauve velvet and draped with silver silk and guar-
anteed weatherproof and wormproof for the sake of a hand-
ful of dust, five fingers of ashes and nobody knows the
trouble I've seen, nobody knows but Jesus.

A modern mortician in a morning coat, or tails and white
tie, let him stand at a door with frozen phizzog, a
mug meant to be solemn, let him welcome the witnesses
to the last rites while a console delivers Rock of Ages,
Cleft for Me, while a hired quartet intones paid-for
grief and calls it nice work if they can get it: let

the black limousines with crepe and insignia follow the
motorized slick glass hearse to the grave where a
slow gray rain drizzles on the mourners: there let an
animated mummy in prinzalbert and tophat pronounce a few
lines:

"She was a star who dropped from her orbit.
"Annie doesn't live here any more.
"Sorry that number is discontinued.
"The deceased was born, had a life of it,
    made her reservations, and is now checked
    out.
"She knew the meaning of meaning and then
    forgot it before she could tell it."

Always in each passing and phantom age
they give her short shrift and a burial.
Under the sod with regrets and embellishments
they lay away a lady in lavender and old lace,
            in arsenic and old lace.
Or again
into the waters of a makebelieve ocean, a painted pretense
of a beneficent and everlasting sea, they fling the sawdust
cadaver of an overstuffed mockery of a beautiful girl made
to be thrown away, a prop, a theater prop, a horselaugh prop
            for the caverns of the briny deep,
            to be rocked in the cradle of the deep,
            locked in the stable with the sheep.

The illusion has gravity and consequences
like a couple of satisfied vaudevillians
            sawing a woman in two:
Watch them closely, she bleeds if mirrors bleed,
            sawing a woman in two.

Let her down easy, boys.
Shovel the dirt in softly.
Hang up a skull-and-crossbones
    with clean eye-sockets and
    a significant grin.
On your honor say no word anywhere
    of the two blue holes in her back
    from an ice-pick.
Or tell it she was one more naked woman

sawed in two and not a dribble of
blood stain for a clue.
Or repeat in a mummy voice: "She was a
star who dropped from her orbit. She
knew the meaning of meaning and then
forgot it before she could tell it."

MEN OF SCIENCE SAY THEIR SAY

men of science say their say:
there will be people left over
enough inhabitants among the Eskimos
among jungle folk
denizens of plains and plateaus
cities and towns synthetic miasma missed
enough for a census
enough to call it still a world
though definitely   my friends   my good friends
definitely not the same old world
the vanquished saying, "What happened?"
the victors saying, "We planned it so."
if it should be at the end
in the smoke   the mist   the silence of the end
if it should be one side lost   the other side won
the changes among those leftover people
the scattered ones the miasma missed
their programs of living   their books and music
they will be simple and conclusive
in the ways and manners of early men and women
the children having playroom
rulers and diplomats finding affairs less complex
new types of cripples here and there
and indescribable babbling survivors
listening to plain scholars saying,
should a few plain scholars have come through,
"As after other wars the peace is something else again."

amid the devastated areas and the untouched
the historians will take an interest

finding amid the ruins and shambles
tokens of contrast and surprise
testimonies here curious   there monstrous
nuclear fission corpses having one face
radioactivity cadavers another look
bacteriological victims not unfamiliar
scenes and outlooks nevertheless surpassing
    those of the First World War
    and those of the Second or Global War
    —the historians will take an interest
    fill their note-books   pick their way
    amid burned and tattered documents
    and say to each other,
    "What the hell! it isn't worth writing,
    posterity won't give a damn what we write."

in the Dark Ages many there and then
had fun and took love and made visions
and listened when Voices came.
then as now were the Unafraid.
then as now, "What if I am dropped into levels
    of ambiguous dust and covered
    over and forgotten? Have I in my
    time taken worse?"
then as now, "What if I am poured into numbers
    of the multitudinous sea and sunk
    in massive swarming fathoms? Have
    I gone through this last year
    and the year before?"
in either Dark Ages or Renascence have there
been ever the Immeasurable Men, the Incalculable
Women, their outlooks timeless?
of Rabelais, is it admissible he threw an excel-
lent laughter and his flagons and ovens made
him a name?
of Piers Plowman, is it permissible he made sad
lovable songs out of stubborn land, straw and
hoe-handles, barefoot folk treading dirt floors?
should it be the Dark Ages recur, will there be
again the Immeasurable Men, the Incalculable
Women?

NAME US A KING

Name us a king
who shall live forever—
a peanut king, a potato king,
a gasket king, a brass-tack king,
a wall-paper king with a wall-paper crown
and a wall-paper queen with wall-paper jewels.

Name us a king
so keen, so fast, so hard,
he shall last forever—
and all the yes-men square shooters
telling the king, "Okay Boss, you shall
        last forever! and then some!"
telling it to an onion king, a pecan king,
a zipper king or a chewing gum king,
any consolidated amalgamated syndicate king—
listening to the yes-men telling him
he shall live forever, he is so keen,
        so fast, so hard,
an okay Boss who shall never bite the dust,
never go down and be a sandwich for the worms
        like us—the customers,
        like us—the customers.

RED AND WHITE

Nobody picks a red rose when the winter wind howls and the
        white snow blows among the fences and storm doors.
Nobody watches the dreamy sculptures of snow when the sum-
        mer roses blow red and soft in the garden yards and
        corners.
O I have loved red roses and O I have loved white snow—
        dreamy drifts winter and summer—roses and snow.

SAYINGS OF HENRY STEPHENS
(Springfield, Illinois, 1917)

If you get enough money
you can buy anything
except . . . you got to die.

I don't like meatheads
shootin' off their mouths
always wrasslin' 'n wranglin'.

The cost of things to live on
has gone too high.
They ought to be brung down
where they's more equal like
with other things.

One summer
potatoes was peddled
around Springfield here
for fifty cents a bushel;
another summer
I paid four dollars a bushel.
Tell me why this is.
We got to work to eat.
And the scripture says:
"Muzzle not the ox that
treadeth out the corn."

Human is human.
Human may be wrong
but it's human all the same.
There's time when a scab
ought to have his head knocked off
his shoulders.
But first we ought to talk to him
like a brother.
I pay a dollar a month to the coal miners' union
to help the street car strikers.
It costs me $25 if they ketch me ridin' on a car.
That's all right.

Las' Monday night I busted somethin' in my left arm.
I walked, mind you, I walked a mile and a half
down to the doctor's office.
It kep' on swellin' an' when I got home
my wife had to put salt and vinegar on
to get my sleeve loose.

They always did say
Springfield is a wickeder town for women
than Chicago.
I see 'em on the streets.
It always was
an' I guess always will be.
Fifty per cent of the men that gets married
makes a mistake.
Why is that?

You're a white man
an' I'm a negro.
Your nationality don't make no difference.
    If I kill you
    Everybody says:
"Henry Stephens, a negro, killed a white man."
I got a little Indian blood in me
but that wouldn't count.

Springfield is Abraham Lincoln's town.
There's only eight mines out of twenty
In Sangamon county
Where the white miners
Let a negro work.

If I buy a house right next to the Peabody mine
That won't do no good.
Only white men digs coal there.
I got to walk a mile, two miles, further,
Where the black man can dig coal.
The United Mine Workers
Is one of the best or-gan-IZ-a-tions there is.
United means union,
And union means united.

But they's mines runnin' twenty-five years
And the white man never lets the negro in.

I remember when we was tryin' to organize.
We met in barns an' holes,
We met in the jungles.
I used to go to all the meetin's them days.
Now we meet downtown in a hall.
Now we's recognized by everybody
Fur one of the most powerful or-gan-IZ-a-tions
in the United States.

I don't go to meetin's nowadays
But if they's a cause to strike for I'll strike.
     I'd live in the fields on hard corn for a just cause.
Yes, for a just cause I'd live in the fields
On hard corn.

AIR CIRCUS

Were there too many revolving mirrors?
Did silver and rose lights cross too often?
Riders came crying: Riddle me this.
Riders straddling gold prongs cried and held on
while trick planes, pursuit and combat planes, bombers
and helicopters, in a bath of beacons came dropping flags—
     And each rider picked up a revolving mirror?
     And each rider twisted in silver and rose?

MADISON AND 42ND

Two taxi drivers stopped for a red light
long enough to refer to a third taxi driver:
     "He likes to be behind the wheel, drives
     seven days a week, takes one day off every
     three months."
     "Yes, I know him. When he dies he'll want
     to take the wheel with him."

INSTRUCTIONS

I commend you to George Washington Hill.
Living, he gave instructions.
Dying, his instructions are remembered.
In billions and zillions he sold cigarettes.
He told the copyrighters and radio gabbers:
      "Irritate 'em! Irritate 'em!
      They'll forget the irritation
      and remember the name of your
      product."
Tell the stonecutters to cut these lines deep
  in the tomb of George Washington Hill.

ALTGELD

Listen to the ticking of the old Great Clock.
John P. Altgeld says the old Great Clock is ticking.
Hammer your way through hell and back and get a million
    dollars.
        What for?
      Backward and forward,
        Day and night,
      Year in, year out,
John P. Altgeld says the old Great Clock is ticking.

WAITING FOR THE CHARIOT
(Mrs. Peter Cartwright)

Can bare fact make the cloth of a shining poem?
In Sangamon County, Illinois, they remembered how
The aged widow walked a mile from home to Bethel Chapel
Where she heard the services and was called on
"To give her testimony," rising to speak freely, ending:
    "The past three weeks have been the happiest
    of all my life; I am waiting for the chariot."
The pastor spoke the benediction; the members rose and moved

Into the aisles toward the door, and looking back
They saw the widow of the famous circuit rider
Sitting quiet and pale in an inviolable dignity
And they heard the pastor: "The chariot has arrived."

WAS EVER A DREAM A DRUM?

Was ever a dream a drum
    or a drum a dream?
Can a drummer drum a dream
    or a dreamer dream a drum?

The drum in a dream
    pounds loud to the dreamer.

Now the moon tonight over Indiana
is a fire-drum of a phantom dreamer.

UNDER THE CAPITOL DOME

There are those who speak of confusion today
as though yesterday there was order
rather than confusion.

There are those who point to confusion today
as though if given a chance
they could tomorrow transform it into order.

There are those who find benefits in confusion
and make it a labor of delight
to render any confusion more confounded.

There are those who expect today's confusion
to be followed by another tomorrow,
these two confusions being different from each other.

The confusions of being born are followed
by the confusions of how to live
until a final moment when a stilled heart
holds release complete and absolute
from all former and earlier confusions.

When one confusion transforms itself into another
there has been a death and a birth
though the newborn confusion
becomes known only across time and silence.

When a confusion results
from *seeing* what is not all there
it is an identical twin of the confusion
to follow the *hearing* of what is not all there.

When a witness says
there was confusion in what he saw
and he can't therefore be sure of what he saw,
he may be a strictly honest witness.

A fine sunrise or an elegant sunset
achieves moving colors and masses of changing light
in a properly organized confusion.

    The orderly marches
of the night stars and constellations
when looked at by powerful telescopes
      hold flagrant and flaming confusions.

ISLE OF PATMOS

    The invisible chariots
    of the tall sky
    must hold archangels
    themselves invisible,
I have seen these chariots.
    So have you

Or you have missed something.
I have talked with archangels.
        So have you
Or you have missed something.
I carry archangels with me
wherever I go. And so do you
or you are missing something.
I am a smoke wisp. So are you.
I need archangels. So do you.
Else you are missing something.
I make archangels as I need them.
        So do you.
Riders we are in white robes, wings,
        Riders of chosen chariots.

Chicago Poems
(1916)

CHICAGO

Hog Butcher for the World,
Tool Maker, Stacker of Wheat,
Player with Railroads and the Nation's Freight Handler;
Stormy, husky, brawling,
City of the Big Shoulders:

They tell me you are wicked and I believe them, for I have
seen your painted women under the gas lamps luring the
farm boys.
And they tell me you are crooked and I answer: Yes, it is true
I have seen the gunman kill and go free to kill again.
And they tell me you are brutal and my reply is: On the faces
of women and children I have seen the marks of wanton
hunger.
And having answered so I turn once more to those who sneer
at this my city, and I give them back the sneer and say to
them:
Come and show me another city with lifted head singing so
proud to be alive and coarse and strong and cunning.
Flinging magnetic curses amid the toil of piling job on job,
here is a tall bold slugger set vivid against the little soft
cities;
Fierce as a dog with tongue lapping for action, cunning as a
savage pitted against the wilderness,
Bareheaded,
Shoveling,
Wrecking,
Planning,
Building, breaking, rebuilding,
Under the smoke, dust all over his mouth, laughing with white
teeth,
Under the terrible burden of destiny laughing as a young man
laughs,
Laughing even as an ignorant fighter laughs who has never lost
a battle,
Bragging and laughing that under his wrist is the pulse, and
under his ribs the heart of the people,
Laughing!

Laughing the stormy, husky, brawling laughter of Youth, half-
    naked, sweating, proud to be Hog Butcher, Tool Maker,
    Stacker of Wheat, Player with Railroads and Freight Han-
    dler to the Nation.

LOST

Desolate and lone
All night long on the lake
Where fog trails and mist creeps,
The whistle of a boat
Calls and cries unendingly,
Like some lost child
In tears and trouble
Hunting the harbor's breast
And the harbor's eyes.

HAPPINESS

I asked professors who teach the meaning of life to tell me what is
    happiness.
And I went to famous executives who boss the work of thousands of
    men.
They all shook their heads and gave me a smile as though I was
    trying to fool with them.
And then one Sunday afternoon I wandered out along the Desplaines
    river
And I saw a crowd of Hungarians under the trees with their women
    and children and a keg of beer and an accordion.

MAG

I wish to God I never saw you, Mag.
I wish you never quit your job and came along with me.
I wish we never bought a license and a white dress
For you to get married in the day we ran off to a minister
And told him we would love each other and take care of each
     other
Always and always long as the sun and the rain lasts anywhere.
Yes, I'm wishing now you lived somewhere away from here
And I was a bum on the bumpers a thousand miles away dead
     broke.
        I wish the kids had never come
        And rent and coal and clothes to pay for
        And a grocery man calling for cash,
        Every day cash for beans and prunes.
        I wish to God I never saw you, Mag.
        I wish to God the kids had never come.

PERSONALITY

Musings of a Police Reporter in the Identification Bureau

You have loved forty women, but you have only one thumb.
You have led a hundred secret lives, but you mark only one
     thumb.
You go round the world and fight in a thousand wars and win
     all the world's honors, but when you come back home the
     print of the one thumb your mother gave you is the same
     print of thumb you had in the old home when your mother
     kissed you and said good-by.
Out of the whirling womb of time come millions of men and
     their feet crowd the earth and they cut one another's
     throats for room to stand and among them all are not two
     thumbs alike.
Somewhere is a Great God of Thumbs who can tell the inside
     story of this.

LIMITED

I am riding on a limited express, one of the crack trains of the
    nation.
Hurtling across the prairie into blue haze and dark air go fifteen
    all-steel coaches holding a thousand people.
(All the coaches shall be scrap and rust and all the men and
    women laughing in the diners and sleepers shall pass to
    ashes.)
I ask a man in the smoker where he is going and he answers:
    "Omaha."

UNDER A HAT RIM

While the hum and the hurry
Of passing footfalls
Beat in my ear like the restless surf
Of a wind-blown sea,
A soul came to me
Out of the look on a face.

Eyes like a lake
Where a storm-wind roams
Caught me from under
The rim of a hat.
    I thought of a midsea wreck
    and bruised fingers clinging
    to a broken state-room door.

CHILD OF THE ROMANS

The dago shovelman sits by the railroad track
Eating a noon meal of bread and bologna.
    A train whirls by, and men and women at tables
    Alive with red roses and yellow jonquils
    Eat steaks running with brown gravy,
    Strawberries and cream, eclairs and coffee.

The dago shovelman finishes the dry bread and bologna,
Washes it down with a dipper from the water-boy,
And goes back to the second half of a ten-hour day's work
Keeping the road-bed so the roses and jonquils
Shake hardly at all in the cut glass vases
Standing slender on the tables in the dining cars.

FOG

The fog comes
on little cat feet.

It sits looking
over harbor and city
on silent haunches
and then moves on.

KILLERS

I am singing to you
Soft as a man with a dead child speaks;
Hard as a man in handcuffs,
Held where he cannot move:

Under the sun
Are sixteen million men,
Chosen for shining teeth,
Sharp eyes, hard legs,
And a running of young warm blood in their wrists.

And a red juice runs on the green grass;
And a red juice soaks the dark soil.
And the sixteen million are killing . . . and killing and killing.

I never forget them day or night:
They beat on my head for memory of them:

They pound on my heart and I cry back to them,
To their homes and women, dreams and games.

I wake in the night and smell the trenches,
And hear the low stir of sleepers in lines—
Sixteen million sleepers and pickets in the dark:
Some of them long sleepers for always,
Some of them tumbling to sleep tomorrow for always,
Fixed in the drag of the world's heartbreak,
Eating and drinking, toiling . . . on a long job of killing.
Sixteen million men.

UNDER THE HARVEST MOON

Under the harvest moon,
When the soft silver
Drips shimmering
Over the garden nights,
Death, the gray mocker,
Comes and whispers to you
As a beautiful friend
Who remembers.

Under the summer roses
When the flagrant crimson
Lurks in the dusk
Of the wild red leaves,
Love, with little hands,
Comes and touches you
With a thousand memories,
And asks you
Beautiful, unanswerable questions.

NOCTURNE IN A DESERTED BRICKYARD

Stuff of the moon
Runs on the lapping sand
Out to the longest shadows.
Under the curving willows,
And round the creep of the wave line,
Fluxions of yellow and dusk on the waters
Make a wide dreaming pansy of an old pond in the night.

THEME IN YELLOW

I spot the hills
With yellow balls in autumn.
I light the prairie cornfields
Orange and tawny gold clusters
And I am called pumpkins.
On the last of October
When dusk is fallen
Children join hands
And circle round me
Singing ghost songs
And love to the harvest moon;
I am a jack-o'-lantern
With terrible teeth
And the children know
I am fooling.

CHILD

The young child, Christ, is straight and wise
And asks questions of the old men, questions
Found under running water for all children
And found under shadows thrown on still waters
By tall trees looking downward, old and gnarled.
Found to the eyes of children alone, untold,
Singing a low song in the loneliness.

And the young child, Christ, goes on asking
And the old men answer nothing and only know love
For the young child. Christ, straight and wise.

GONE

Everybody loved Chick Lorimer in our town.
            Far off
            Everybody loved her.
So we all love a wild girl keeping a hold
            On a dream she wants.
Nobody knows now where Chick Lorimer went.
Nobody knows why she packed her trunk . . . a few old things
And is gone,
                  Gone with her little chin
                  Thrust ahead of her
                  And her soft hair blowing careless
                  From under a wide hat,
Dancer, singer, a laughing passionate lover.

Were there ten men or a hundred hunting Chick?
Were there five men or fifty with aching hearts?
            Everybody loved Chick Lorimer.
            Nobody knows where she's gone.

UNDER A TELEPHONE POLE

I am a copper wire slung in the air,
Slim against the sun I make not even a clear line of shadow.
Night and day I keep singing—humming and thrumming:
It is love and war and money; it is the fighting and the tears,
    the work and want,
Death and laughter of men and women passing through me,
    carrier of your speech,
In the rain and the wet dripping, in the dawn and the shine
    drying,
            A copper wire.

Cornhuskers
(1918)

From PRAIRIE

I was born on the prairie and the milk of its wheat, the red of
its clover, the eyes of its women, gave me a song and a
slogan.

Here the water went down, the icebergs slid with gravel, the
gaps and the valleys hissed, and the black loam came, and
the yellow sandy loam.
Here between the sheds of the Rocky Mountains and the Ap-
palachians, here now a morning star fixes a fire sign over
the timber claims and cow pastures, the corn belt, the
cotton belt, the cattle ranches.
Here the gray geese go five hundred miles and back with a
wind under their wings honking the cry for a new home.
Here I know I will hanker after nothing so much as one more
sunrise or a sky moon of fire doubled to a river moon of
water.

The prairie sings to me in the forenoon and I know in the
night I rest easy in the prairie arms, on the prairie heart.

.   .   .   .

I am the prairie, mother of men, waiting.
They are mine, the threshing crews eating beefsteak, the farm-
boys driving steers to the railroad cattle pens.
They are mine, the crowds of people at a Fourth of July basket
picnic, listening to a lawyer read the Declaration of Inde-
pendence, watching the pinwheels and Roman candles at
night, the young men and women two by two hunting the
bypaths and kissing-bridges.
They are mine, the horses looking over a fence in the frost of
late October saying good morning to the horses hauling
wagons of rutabaga to market.
They are mine, the old zigzag rail fences, the new barbwire.

.   .   .

The cornhuskers wear leather on their hands.
There is no let-up to the wind.
Blue bandanas are knotted at the ruddy chins.

Falltime and winter apples take on the smolder of the five-o'clock
    November sunset: falltime, leaves, bonfires, stubble, the
    old things go, and the earth is grizzled.
The land and the people hold memories, even among the anthills
    and the angleworms, among the toads and woodroaches—
    among gravestone writings rubbed out by the rain—they
    keep old things that never grow old.

The frost loosens cornhusks.
The sun, the rain, the wind
            loosen cornhusks.
The men and women are helpers.
They are all cornhuskers together.
I see them late in the western evening
            in a smoke-red dust.

.   .   .   .

O prairie mother, I am one of your boys.
I have loved the prairie as a man with a heart shot full of pain
    over love.
Here I know I will hanker after nothing so much as one more
    sunrise or a sky moon of fire doubled to a river moon of
    water.

               . . .

I speak of new cities and new people.
I tell you the past is a bucket of ashes.
I tell you yesterday is a wind gone down,
    a sun dropped in the west.
I tell you there is nothing in the world
    only an ocean of tomorrows,
    a sky of tomorrows.

I am a brother of the cornhuskers who say
    at sundown:
            Tomorrow is a day.

LAUGHING CORN

There was a high majestic fooling
Day before yesterday in the yellow corn.

And day after tomorrow in the yellow corn
There will be high majestic fooling.

The ears ripen in late summer
And come on with a conquering laughter,
Come on with a high and conquering laughter.

The long-tailed blackbirds are hoarse.
One of the smaller blackbirds chitters on a stalk
And a spot of red is on its shoulder
And I never heard its name in my life.

Some of the ears are bursting.
A white juice works inside.
Cornsilk creeps in the end and dangles in the wind.
Always—I never knew it any other way—
The wind and the corn talk things over together.
And the rain and the corn and the sun and the corn
Talk things over together.

Over the road is the farmhouse.
The siding is white and a green blind is slung loose.
It will not be fixed till the corn is husked.
The farmer and his wife talk things over together.

WILDERNESS

There is a wolf in me . . . fangs pointed for tearing gashes . . .
a red tongue for raw meat . . . and the hot lapping of
blood—I keep this wolf because the wilderness gave it to
me and the wilderness will not let it go.

There is a fox in me . . . a silver-gray fox . . . I sniff and guess
. . . I pick things out of the wind and air . . . I nose in the
dark night and take sleepers and eat them and hide the
feathers . . . I circle and loop and double-cross.

There is a hog in me . . . a snout and a belly . . . a machinery
for eating and grunting . . . a machinery for sleeping satis-
fied in the sun—I got this too from the wilderness and the
wilderness will not let it go.

There is a fish in me . . . I know I came from salt-blue water-
gates . . . I scurried with shoals of herring . . . I blew
waterspouts with porpoises . . . before land was . . . before
the water went down . . . before Noah . . . before the first
chapter of Genesis.

There is a baboon in me . . . clambering-clawed . . . dog-
faced . . . yawping a galoot's hunger . . . hairy under the
armpits . . . here are the hawk-eyed hankering men . . .
here are the blonde and blue-eyed women . . . here they
hide curled asleep waiting . . . ready to snarl and kill . . .
ready to sing and give milk . . . waiting—I keep the baboon
because the wilderness says so.

There is an eagle in me and a mockingbird . . . and the eagle
flies among the Rocky Mountains of my dreams and fights
among the Sierra crags of what I want . . . and the
mockingbird warbles in the early forenoon before the dew
is gone, warbles in the underbrush of my Chattanoogas of
hope, gushes over the blue Ozark foothills of my wishes
—And I got the eagle and the mockingbird from the
wilderness.

I got a zoo, I got a menagerie, inside my ribs, under my
bony head, under my red-valve heart—and I got some-
thing else: it is a man-child heart, a woman-child heart:
it is a father and mother and lover: it came from God-
Knows-Where: it is going to God-Knows Where—For I
am the keeper of the zoo: I say yes and no: I sing and
kill and work: I am a pal of the world: I came from the
wilderness.

FIRE-LOGS

Nancy Hanks dreams by the fire;
Dreams, and the logs sputter,
And the yellow tongues climb.
Red lines lick their way in flickers.
Oh, sputter, logs.
    Oh, dream, Nancy.
Time now for a beautiful child.
Time now for a tall man to come.

SOUTHERN PACIFIC

Huntington sleeps in a house six feet long.
Huntington dreams of railroads he built and owned.
Huntington dreams of ten thousand men saying: Yes, sir.

Blithery sleeps in a house six feet long.
Blithery dreams of rails and ties he laid.
Blithery dreams of saying to Huntington: Yes, sir.

Huntington,
Blithery, sleep in houses six feet long.

BUFFALO BILL

Boy heart of Johnny Jones—aching today?
Aching, and Buffalo Bill in town?
Buffalo Bill and ponies, cowboys, Indians?

Some of us know
All about it, Johnny Jones.
Buffalo Bill is a slanting look of the eyes.
  A slanting look under a hat on a horse.
He sits on a horse and a passing look is fixed

On Johnny Jones, you and me, barelegged,
A slanting, passing, careless look under a hat on a horse.

Go clickety-clack, O pony hoofs along the street.
Come on and slant your eyes again, O Buffalo Bill.
Give us again the ache of our boy hearts.
Fill us again with the red love of prairies, dark nights, lonely
    wagons, and the crack-crack of rifles sputtering flashes
    into an ambush.

PRAYERS OF STEEL

Lay me on an anvil, O God.
Beat me and hammer me into a crowbar.
Let me pry loose old walls.
Let me lift and loosen old foundations.

Lay me on an anvil, O God.
Beat me and hammer me into a steel spike.
Drive me into the girders that hold a skyscraper together.
Take red-hot rivets and fasten me into the central girders.
Let me be the great nail holding a skyscraper through blue
    nights into white stars.

PSALM OF THOSE WHO GO FORTH
BEFORE DAYLIGHT

The policeman buys shoes slow and careful; the teamster buys
    gloves slow and careful; they take care of their feet and
    hands; they live on their feet and hands.

The milkman never argues; he works alone and no one speaks
    to him; the city is asleep when he is on the job; he puts a
    bottle on six hundred porches and calls it a day's work;
    he climbs two hundred wooden stairways; two horses are
    company for him; he never argues.

The rolling-mill men and the sheet-steel men are brothers of
cinders; they empty cinders out of their shoes after the
day's work; they ask their wives to fix burnt holes in the
knees of their trousers; their necks and ears are covered
with a smut; they scour their necks and ears; they are
brothers of cinders.

COOL TOMBS

When Abraham Lincoln was shoveled into the tombs, he forgot
the copperheads and the assassin . . . in the dust, in the
cool tombs.

And Ulysses Grant lost all thought of con men and Wall Street,
cash and collateral turned ashes . . . in the dust, in the cool
tombs.

Pocahontas' body, lovely as a poplar, sweet as a red haw in
November or a pawpaw in May, did she wonder? does she
remember? . . . in the dust, in the cool tombs?

Take any streetful of people buying clothes and groceries, cheer-
ing a hero or throwing confetti and blowing tin horns . . .
tell me if the lovers are losers . . . tell me if any get more
than the lovers . . . in the dust . . . in the cool tombs.

GRASS

Pile the bodies high at Austerlitz and Waterloo.
Shovel them under and let me work—
                    I am the grass; I cover all.

And pile them high at Gettysburg
And pile them high at Ypres and Verdun.
Shovel them under and let me work.
Two years, ten years, and passengers ask the conductor:

What place is this?
Where are we now?

I am the grass.
Let me work.

Smoke and Steel
(1920)

From SMOKE AND STEEL

   A bar of steel—it is only
Smoke at the heart of it, smoke and the blood of a man.
A runner of fire ran in it, ran out, ran somewhere else,
And left—smoke and the blood of a man
And the finished steel, chilled and blue.
So fire runs in, runs out, runs somewhere else again,
And the bar of steel is a gun, a wheel, a nail, a shovel,
A rudder under the sea, a steering-gear in the sky;
And always dark in the heart and through it,
   Smoke and the blood of a man.
Pittsburgh, Youngstown, Gary—they make their steel with men.

In the blood of men and the ink of chimneys
The smoke nights write their oaths:
Smoke into steel and blood into steel;
Homestead, Braddock, Birmingham, they make their steel with
  men.
Smoke and blood is the mix of steel.

   The birdmen drone
   in the blue; it is steel
   a motor sings and zooms.

RED-HEADED RESTAURANT CASHIER

Shake back your hair, O red-headed girl.
Let go your laughter and keep your two proud freckles on your
  chin.
Somewhere is a man looking for a red-headed girl and some day
  maybe he will look into your eyes for a restaurant cashier
  and find a lover, maybe.
Around and around go ten thousand men hunting a red-headed
  girl with two freckles on her chin.
I have seen them hunting, hunting.
   Shake back your hair; let go your laughter.

CLEAN CURTAINS

New neighbors came to the corner house at Congress and Green
streets.

The look of their clean white curtains was the same as the rim
of a nun's bonnet.

One way was an oyster pail factory, one way they made candy,
one way paper boxes, strawboard cartons.
The warehouse trucks shook the dust of the ways loose and the
wheels whirled dust—there was dust of hoof and wagon
wheel and rubber tire—dust of police and fire wagons—
dust of the winds that circled at midnights and noon lis-
tening to no prayers.

"O mother, I know the heart of you," I sang passing the rim of
a nun's bonnet—O white curtains—and people clean as the
prayers of Jesus here in the faded ramshackle at Congress
and Green.

Dust and the thundering trucks won—the barrages of the street
wheels and the lawless wind took their way—was it five
weeks or six the little mother, the new neighbors, battled
and then took away the white prayers in the windows?

THE HANGMAN AT HOME

What does the hangman think about
When he goes home at night from work?
When he sits down with his wife and
Children for a cup of coffee and a
Plate of ham and eggs, do they ask
Him if it was a good day's work
And everything went well or do they
Stay off some topics and talk about
The weather, baseball, politics
And the comic strips in the papers

And the movies? Do they look at his
Hands when he reaches for the coffee
Or the ham and eggs? If the little
Ones say, Daddy, play horse, here's
A rope—does he answer like a joke:
I seen enough rope for today?
Or does his face light up like a
Bonfire of joy and does he say:
It's a good and dandy world we live
In. And if a white face moon looks
In through a window where a baby girl
Sleeps and the moon-gleams mix with
Baby ears and baby hair—the hangman—
How does he act then? It must be easy
For him. Anything is easy for a hangman,
I guess.

BROKEN-FACE GARGOYLES

All I can give you is broken-face gargoyles.
It is too early to sing and dance at funerals,
Though I can whisper to you I am looking for an undertaker
    humming a lullaby and throwing his feet in a swift and
    mystic buck-and-wing, now you see it and now you don't.

Fish to swim a pool in your garden flashing a speckled silver,
A basket of wine-saps filling your room with flame-dark for
    your eyes and the tang of valley orchards for your nose,
Such a beautiful pail of fish, such a beautiful peck of apples,
    I cannot bring you now.
It is too early and I am not footloose yet.

I shall come in the night when I come with a hammer and saw.
I shall come near your window, where you look out when your
    eyes open in the morning.
And there I shall slam together bird-houses and bird-baths for
    wing-loose wrens and hummers to live in, birds with yel-
    low wing tips to blur and buzz soft all summer,
So I shall make little fool homes with doors, always open doors
    for all and each to run away when they want to.

I shall come just like that even though now it is early and I am
not yet footloose,
Even though I am still looking for an undertaker with a raw,
wind-bitten face and a dance in his feet.
I make a date with you (put it down) for six o'clock in the
evening a thousand years from now.

All I can give you now is broken-face gargoyles.
All I can give you now is a double gorilla head with two
fish mouths and four eagle eyes hooked on a street wall,
spouting water and looking two ways to the ends of the
street for the new people, the young strangers, coming,
coming, always coming.

It is early.

DEATH SNIPS PROUD MEN

Death is stronger than all the governments because the govern-
ments are men and men die and then death laughs: Now
you see 'em, now you don't.

Death is stronger than all proud men and so death snips proud
men on the nose, throws a pair of dice and says: Read 'em
and weep.

Death sends a radiogram every day: When I want you I'll drop
in—and then one day he comes with a master-key and lets
himself in and says: We'll go now.

Death is a nurse mother with big arms: 'Twon't hurt you at all;
it's your time now; you just need a long sleep, child;
what have you had anyhow better than sleep?

JAZZ FANTASIA

Drum on your drums, batter on your banjoes,
sob on the long cool winding saxophones.
Go to it, O jazzmen.

Sling your knuckles on the bottoms of the happy
tin pans, let your trombones ooze, and go husha-
husha-hush with the slippery sand-paper.

Moan like an autumn wind high in the lonesome treetops, moan
soft like you wanted somebody terrible, cry like a racing car
slipping away from a motorcycle cop, bang-bang! you jazzmen,
bang altogether drums, traps, banjoes, horns, tin cans—make
two people fight on the top of a stairway and scratch each other's
eyes in a clinch tumbling down the stairs.

Can the rough stuff . . . now a Mississippi steamboat pushes up
the night river with a hoo-hoo-hoo-oo . . . and the green lanterns
calling to the high soft stars . . . a red moon rides on the humps
of the low river hills . . . go to it, O jazzmen.

FOUR PRELUDES ON PLAYTHINGS
OF THE WIND
"The past is a bucket of ashes."

1

The woman named Tomorrow
sits with a hairpin in her teeth
and takes her time
and does her hair the way she wants it
and fastens at last the last braid and coil
and puts the hairpin where it belongs
and turns and drawls: Well, what of it?
My grandmother, Yesterday, is gone.
What of it? Let the dead be dead.

2

The doors were cedar
and the panels strips of gold
and the girls were golden girls
and the panels read and the girls chanted:
    We are the greatest city,
    the greatest nation:
    nothing like us ever was.
The doors are twisted on broken hinges.
Sheets of rain swish through on the wind
        where the golden girls ran and the panels read:
    We are the greatest city,
    the greatest nation,
    nothing like us ever was.

3

It has happened before.
Strong men put up a city and got
        a nation together,
And paid singers to sing and women
        to warble: We are the greatest city,
                the greatest nation,
                nothing like us ever was.

And while the singers sang
and the strong men listened
and paid the singers well
and felt good about it all,
    there were rats and lizards who listened
    . . . and the only listeners left now
    . . . are . . . the rats . . . and the lizards.

And there are black crows
crying, "Caw, caw,"
bringing mud and sticks
building a nest
over the words carved
on the doors where the panels were cedar
and the strips on the panels were gold
and the golden girls came singing:
    We are the greatest city,
    the greatest nation:
    nothing like us ever was.

The only singers now are crows crying, "Caw, caw,"
And the sheets of rain whine in the wind and doorways.
And the only listeners now are . . . the rats . . . and
    the lizards.

4

The feet of the rats
scribble on the doorsills;
the hieroglyphs of the rat footprints
chatter the pedigrees of the rats
and babble of the blood
and gabble of the breed
of the grandfathers and the great-grandfathers
of the rats.

And the wind shifts
and the dust on a doorsill shifts
and even the writing of the rat footprints
tells us nothing, nothing at all
about the greatest city, the greatest nation
where the strong men listened
and the women warbled: Nothing like us ever was.

THREES

I was a boy when I heard three red words
a thousand Frenchmen died in the streets
for: Liberty, Equality, Fraternity—I asked
why men die for words.

I was older; men with mustaches, sideburns,
lilacs, told me the high golden words are:
Mother, Home, and Heaven—other older men with
face decorations said: God, Duty, Immortality
—they sang these threes slow from deep lungs.

Years ticked off their say-so on the great clocks
of doom and damnation, soup and nuts: meteors flashed

their say-so: and out of great Russia came three
dusky syllables workmen took guns and went out to die
for: Bread, Peace, Land.

And I met a marine of the U.S.A., a leatherneck with a girl on
his knee for a memory in ports circling the earth and he said:
Tell me how to say three things and I always get by—gimme
a plate of ham and eggs—how much?—and—do you love me,
kid?

A . E . F .

There will be a rusty gun on the wall, sweetheart,
The rifle grooves curling with flakes of rust.
A spider will make a silver string nest in the
            darkest, warmest corner of it.
The trigger and the range-finder, they too will be rusty.
And no hands will polish the gun, and it will hang on the wall.
Forefingers and thumbs will point absently and casually toward
      it.
It will be spoken among half-forgotten, wished-to-be-forgotten
      things.
They will tell the spider: Go on, you're doing good work.

S E A - W A S H

The sea-wash never ends.
The sea-wash repeats, repeats.
Only old songs? Is that all the sea knows?
            Only the old strong songs?
            Is that all?
The sea-wash repeats, repeats.

WIND SONG

Long ago I learned how to sleep,
In an old apple orchard where the wind swept by counting its money
    and throwing it away,
In a wind-gaunt orchard where the limbs forked out and listened or
    never listened at all,
In a passel of trees where the branches trapped the wind into whis-
    tling, "Who, who are you?"
I slept with my head in an elbow on a summer afternoon and there I
    took a sleep lesson.
There I went away saying: I know why they sleep, I know how they
    trap the tricky winds.
Long ago I learned how to listen to the singing wind and how to
    forget and how to hear the deep whine,
Slapping and lapsing under the day blue and the night stars:
        Who, who are you?

        Who can ever forget
        listening to the wind go by
        counting its money
        and throwing it away?

NIGHT STUFF

Listen a while, the moon is a lovely woman, a lonely woman, lost
    in a silver dress, lost in a circus rider's silver dress.

Listen a while, the lake by night is a lonely woman, a lovely
    woman, circled with birches and pines mixing their green and
    white among stars shattered in spray clear nights.

I know the moon and the lake have twisted the roots under my heart
    the same as a lonely woman, a lovely woman, in a silver dress,
    in a circus rider's silver dress.

HAZE

Keep a red heart of memories
Under the great gray rain sheds of the sky,
Under the open sun and the yellow gloaming embers.
Remember all paydays of lilacs and songbirds;
All starlights of cool memories on storm paths.

Out of this prairie rise the faces of dead men.
They speak to me. I can not tell you what they say.

Other faces rise on the prairie.
                              They are the unborn. The future.

Yesterday and tomorrow cross and mix on the skyline.
The two are lost in a purple haze. One forgets. One waits.

In the yellow dust of sunsets, in the meadows of vermilion
        eight o'clock June nights . . . the dead men and the unborn
        children speak to me . . . I can not tell you what they say
        . . . you listen and you know.

I don't care who you are, man:
I know a woman is looking for you
And her soul is a corn-tassel kissing a south-west wind.

(The farm-boy whose face is the color of brick-dust, is calling
        the cows; he will form the letter X with crossed streams of
        milk from the teats; he will beat a tattoo on the bottom of
        a tin pail with X's of milk.)

I don't care who you are, man:
I know sons and daughters looking for you
And they are gray dust working toward star paths
And you see them from a garret window when you laugh
At your luck and murmur, "I don't care."

I don't care who you are, woman:
I know a man is looking for you
And his soul is a south-west wind kissing a corn-tassel.

(The kitchen girl on the farm is throwing oats to the chickens
and the buff of their feathers says hello to the sunset's late
maroon.)

I don't care who you are, woman:
I know sons and daughters looking for you
And they are next year's wheat or the year after hidden in the
dark and loam.

My love is a yellow hammer spinning circles in Ohio, Indiana.
My love is a redbird shooting flights in straight lines in
Kentucky and Tennessee. My love is an early robin flaming
an ember of copper on her shoulders in March and April.
My love is a graybird living in the eaves of a Michigan
house all winter. Why is my love always a crying thing of
wings?

On the Indiana dunes, in the Mississippi marshes, I have asked:
Is it only a fishbone on the beach?
Is it only a dog's jaw or a horse's skull whitening in the sun? Is
the red heart of man only ashes? Is the flame of it all a
white light switched off and the power-house wires cut?

Why do the prairie roses answer every summer? Why do the
changing repeating rains come back out of the salt sea wind-
blown? Why do the stars keep their tracks? Why do the
cradles of the sky rock new babies?

FOR YOU

The peace of great doors be for you.
Wait at the knobs, at the panel oblongs.
Wait for the great hinges.

The peace of great churches be for you,
Where the players of loft pipe organs
Practice old lovely fragments, alone.

The peace of great books be for you,
Stains of pressed clover leaves on pages,
Bleach of the light of years held in leather.

The peace of great prairies be for you.
Listen among windplayers in cornfields,
The wind learning over its oldest music.

The peace of great seas be for you.
Wait on a hook of land, a rock footing
For you, wait in the salt wash.

The peace of great mountains be for you,
The sleep and the eyesight of eagles,
Sheet mist shadows and the long look across.

The peace of great hearts be for you,
Valves of the blood of the sun,
Pumps of the strongest wants we cry.

The peace of great silhouettes be for you,
Shadow dancers alive in your blood now,
Alive and crying, "Let us out, let us out."

The peace of great changes be for you.
Whisper, Oh beginners in the hills.
Tumble, Oh cubs—tomorrow belongs to you.

The peace of great loves be for you.
Rain, soak these roots; wind, shatter the dry rot
Bars of sunlight, grips of the earth, hug these.

The peace of great ghosts be for you,
Phantoms of night-gray eyes, ready to go
To the fog-star dumps, to the fire-white doors.

Yes, the peace of great phantoms be for you,
Phantom iron men, mothers of bronze,
Keepers of the lean clean breeds.

Slabs of the Sunburnt West
(1922)

From THE WINDY CITY

The lean hands of wagon men
put out pointing fingers here,
picked this crossway, put it on a map,
set up their sawbucks, fixed their shotguns,
found a hitching place for the pony express,
made a hitching place for the iron horse,
the one-eyed horse with the fire-spit head,
found a homelike spot and said, "Make a home,"
saw this corner with a mesh of rails, shuttling
 people, shunting cars, shaping the junk of
 the earth to a new city.

The hands of men took hold and tugged
And the breaths of men went into the junk
And the junk stood up into skyscrapers and asked:
Who am I? Am I a city? And if I am what is my name?
And once while the time whistles blew and blew again
The men answered: Long ago we gave you a name,
Long ago we laughed and said: You? Your name is Chicago.

Early the red men gave a name to a river,
 the place of the skunk,
 the river of the wild onion smell,
 Shee-caw-go.

Out of the payday songs of steam shovels,
Out of the wages of structural iron rivets,
The living lighted skyscrapers tell it now as a name,
Tell it across miles of sea blue water, gray blue land:
I am Chicago, I am a name given out by the breaths of work-
 ing men, laughing men, a child, a belonging.

So between the Great Lakes,
The Grand De Tour, and the Grand Prairie,
The living lighted skyscrapers stand,
Spotting the blue dusk with checkers of yellow,

streamers of smoke and silver,
    parallelograms of night gray watchmen,
Singing a soft moaning song: I am a child, a belonging.

.   .   .   .

Put the city up; tear the city down;
    put it up again; let us find a city.
Let us remember the little violet-eyed
    man who gave all, praying, "Dig and
    dream, dream and hammer, till your
    city comes."

Every day the people sleep and the city dies;
    every day the people shake loose, awake and
    build the city again.
The city is a tool chest opened every day,
    a time clock punched every morning,
    a shop door, bunkers and overalls
    counting every day.

The city is a balloon and a bubble plaything
    shot to the sky every evening, whistled in
    a ragtime jig down the sunset.

The city is made, forgotten, and made again,
    trucks hauling it away haul it back
    steered by drivers whistling ragtime
    against the sunsets.

Every day the people get up and carry the city,
    carry the bunkers and balloons of the city,
    lift it and put it down.

.   .   .   .

Winds of the Windy City, come out of the prairie,
    all the way from Medicine Hat.
Come out of the inland sea blue water, come where
    they nickname a city for you.

Corn wind in the fall, come off the black lands,
    come off the whisper of the silk hangers,
    the lap of the flat spear leaves.

Blue water wind in summer, come off the blue miles
    of lake, carry your inland sea blue fingers,
    carry us cool, carry your blue to our homes.

White spring winds, come off the bag wool clouds,
    come off the running melted snow, come white
    as the arms of snow-born children.

Gray fighting winter winds, come along on the tear-
    ing blizzard tails, the snouts of the hungry
    hunting storms, come fighting gray in winter.

Winds of the Windy City,
Winds of corn and sea blue,
Spring wind white and fighting winter gray,
Come home here—they nickname a city for you.

The wind of the lake shore waits and wanders.
The heave of the shore wind hunches the sand piles.
The winkers of the morning stars count out cities
And forget the numbers.

WASHINGTON MONUMENT BY NIGHT

1

The stone goes straight.
A lean swimmer dives into night sky,
Into half-moon mist.

2

Two trees are coal black.
This is a great white ghost between.
It is cool to look at.
Strong men, strong women, come here.

3

Eight years is a long time
To be fighting all the time.

4

The republic is a dream.
Nothing happens unless first a dream.

5

The wind bit hard at Valley Forge one Christmas.
Soldiers tied rags on their feet.
Red footprints wrote on the snow . . .
. . . and stone shoots into stars here
. . . into half-moon mist tonight.

6

Tongues wrangled dark at a man.
He buttoned his overcoat and stood alone.
In a snowstorm, red hollyberries, thoughts,
        he stood alone.

UPSTREAM

    The strong men keep coming on.
    They go down shot, hanged, sick,
            broken.
    They live on fighting, singing,
            lucky as plungers.
    The strong mothers pulling them
            on . . .
    The strong mothers pulling them
            from a dark sea, a great prairie,
            a long mountain.
    Call hallelujah, call amen, call
            deep thanks.
    The strong men keep coming on.

AT THE GATES OF TOMBS

Civilizations are set up and knocked down
the same as pins in a bowling alley.

Civilizations get into the garbage wagons
and are hauled away the same as potato
peelings or any pot scrapings.

Civilizations, all the work of the artists,
inventors, dreamers of work and genius,
go to the dumps one by one.

Be silent about it; since at the gates of tombs
silence is a gift, be silent; since at the epitaphs
written in the air, since at the swan songs hung in
the air, silence is a gift, be silent; forget it.

If any fool, babbler, gabby mouth, stand up and say:
Let us make a civilization where the sacred and
beautiful things of toil and genius shall last—

If any such noisy gazook stands up and makes himself
heard—put him out—tie a can on him—lock him up
in Leavenworth—shackle him in the Atlanta hoosegow
—let him eat from the tin dishes at Sing Sing—
slew him in as a lifer at San Quentin.

It is the law; as a civilization dies and goes down
to eat ashes along with all other dead civilizations
—it is the law all dirty wild dreamers die first—
gag 'em, lock 'em up, get 'em bumped off.

And since at the gates of tombs silence is a gift,
be silent about it, yes, be silent—forget it.

IMPROVED FARM LAND

Tall timber stood here once, here on a corn belt farm along the
Monon.

Here the roots of a half mile of trees dug their runners deep in
the loam for a grip and a hold against wind storms.

Then the axmen came and the chips flew to the zing of steel
and handle—the lank railsplitters cut the big ones first,
the beeches and the oaks, then the brush.

Dynamite, wagons and horses took the stumps—the plows sunk
their teeth in—now it is first class corn land—improved
property—and the hogs grunt over the fodder crops.

It would come hard now for this half mile of improved farm
land along the Monon corn belt, on a piece of Grand
Prairie, to remember once it had a great singing family of
trees.

PRIMER LESSON

Look out how you use proud words.
When you let proud words go, it is
        not easy to call them back.
They wear long boots, hard boots; they
        walk off proud; they can't hear you
        calling—
Look out how you use proud words.

Good Morning, America
(1928)

NINE TENTATIVE (FIRST MODEL) DEFINITIONS OF POETRY

1   *Poetry is a projection across silence of cadences arranged to break that silence with definite intentions of echoes, syllables, wave lengths.*

2   *Poetry is the harnessing of the paradox of earth cradling life and then entombing it.*

3   *Poetry is a series of explanations of life, fading off into horizons too swift for explanations.*

4   *Poetry is a sky dark with a wild-duck migration.*

5   *Poetry is a search for syllables to shoot at the barriers of the unknown and the unknowable.*

6   *Poetry is a packsack of invisible keepsakes.*

7   *Poetry is a phantom script telling how rainbows are made and why they go away.*

8   *Poetry is the achievement of the synthesis of hyacinths and biscuits.*

9   *Poetry is the capture of a picture, a song, or a flair, in a deliberate prism of words.*

From GOOD MORNING, AMERICA

In the evening there is a sunset sonata comes to the cities.
There is a march of little armies to the dwindling of drums.
The skyscrapers throw their tall lengths of walls into black bastions
    on the red west.
The skyscrapers fasten their perpendicular alphabets far across the
    changing silver triangles of stars and streets.

And who made 'em? Who made the skyscrapers?
Man made 'em, the little two-legged joker, Man.
Out of his head, out of his dreaming, scheming skypiece,

Out of proud little diagrams that danced softly in his head—Man
　　made the skyscrapers.
With his two hands, with shovels, hammers, wheelbarrows, with
　　engines, conveyors, signal whistles, with girders, molds, steel,
　　concrete—
Climbing on scaffolds and falsework with blueprints, riding the
　　beams and dangling in mid-air to call, Come on, boys—
　　　　　　　　　　Man made the skyscrapers.

When one tall skyscraper is torn down
To make room for a taller one to go up,
Who takes down and puts up those two skyscrapers?
Man . . . the little two-legged joker . . . Man.

　.　　.　　.　　.　　.　　.　　.　　.　　.　　.　　.　　.

First come the pioneers, lean, hungry, fierce, dirty.
They wrangle and battle with the elements.
They gamble on crops, chills, ague, rheumatism.
They fight wars and put a nation on the map.
They battle with blizzards, lice, wolves.
They go on a fighting trail
To break sod for unnumbered millions to come.

Then the fat years arrive when the fat drips.
Then come the rich men baffled by their riches,
Bewildered by the silence of their tall possessions.
Then come the criers of the ancient desperate taunt:
　　Stuff your guts
　　and strut your stuff,
　　strut it high and handsome;
　　when you die you're dead
　　and there's no comeback
　　and not even the winds
　　will say your name—
　　feed, oh pigs, feed, oh swine.

Old timer, dust of the earth so kindly,
Old timer, dirt of our feet and days.
Old time gravel and gumbo of the earth,
Take them back kindly,
These pigs, these swine.
The bones of them and their brothers blanch to the same yellow of
　　the years.

.   .   .   .

The silent litany of the workmen goes on—
Speed, speed, we are the makers of speed.
We make the flying, crying motors,
Clutches, brakes, and axles,
Gears, ignitions, accelerators,
Spokes and springs and shock absorbers.
The silent litany of the workmen goes on—
Speed, speed, we are the makers of speed;
Axles, clutches, levers, shovels,
We make the signals and lay the way—
     Speed, speed.
The trees come down to our tools.
We carve the wood to the wanted shape.
The whining propeller's song in the sky,
The steady drone of the overland truck,
Comes from our hands; us; the makers of speed.

Speed; the turbines crossing the Big Pond,
Every nut and bolt, every bar and screw,
Every fitted and whirling shaft,
They came from us, the makers,
Us, who know how,
Us, the high designers and the automatic feeders,
Us, with heads,
Us, with hands,
Us, on the long haul, the short flight,
We are the makers; lay the blame on us—
The makers of speed.

.   .   .   .

Sea sunsets, give us keepsakes.
Prairie gloamings, pay us for prayers.
Mountain clouds on bronze skies—
     Give us great memories.
Let us have summer roses.
Let us have tawny harvest haze in pumpkin time.
Let us have springtime faces to toil for and play for.
Let us have the fun of booming winds on long waters.
Give us dreamy blue twilights—of winter evenings—to wrap us in
     a coat of dreaminess.

Moonlight, come down—shine down, moonlight—meet every bird
   cry and every song calling to a hard old earth, a sweet young
   earth.

BABY SONG OF THE FOUR WINDS

Let me be your baby, south wind.
Rock me, let me rock, rock me now.
Rock me low, rock me warm.
Let me be your baby.

Comb my hair, west wind.
Comb me with a cowlick.
Or let me go with a pompadour.
Come on, west wind, make me your baby.

North wind, shake me where I'm foolish.
Shake me loose and change my ways.
Cool my ears with a blue sea wind.
I'm your baby, make me behave.

And you, east wind, what can I ask?
A fog comfort? A fog to tuck me in?
Fix me so and let me sleep.
I'm your baby—and I always was.

BLOSSOM THEMES

1

Late in the winter came one day
When there was a whiff on the wind,
a suspicion, a cry not to be heard
      of perhaps blossoms, perhaps green
      grass and clean hills lifting roll-
      ing shoulders.
Does the nose get the cry of spring
      first of all? is the nose thankful
      and thrilled first of all?

2

If the blossoms come down
so they must fall on snow
because spring comes this year
before winter is gone,
then both snow and blossoms look sad;
peaches, cherries, the red summer apples,
all say it is a hard year.
The wind has its own way of picking off
the smell of peach blossoms and then
carrying that smell miles and miles.
> Women washing dishes in lonely farmhouses
> stand at the door and say, "Something is
> happening."
A little foam of the summer sea
> of blossoms,
> a foam finger of white leaves,
> shut these away—
> high into the summer wind runners.
Let the wind be white too.

SMALL HOMES

The green bug sleeps in the white lily ear.
The red bug sleeps in the white magnolia.
Shiny wings, you are choosers of color.
You have taken your summer bungalows wisely.

SUNSETS

There are sunsets who whisper a good-by.
It is a short dusk and a way for stars.
Prairie and sea rim they go level and even
And the sleep is easy.

There are sunsets who dance good-by.
They fling scarves half to the arc,

To the arc then and over the arc.
Ribbons at the ears, sashes at the hips,
Dancing, dancing good-by. And here sleep
Tosses a little with dreams.

SPLINTER

The voice of the last cricket
across the first frost
is one kind of good-by.
It is so thin a splinter of singing.

A COUPLE

He was in Cincinnati, she in Burlington.
He was in a gang of Postal Telegraph linemen.
She was a pot rassler in a boarding house.
"The crying is lonely," she wrote him.
"The same here," he answered.
The winter went by and he came back and they married.
And he went away again where rainstorms knocked down tele-
        graph poles and wires dropped with frozen sleet.
And again she wrote him, "The crying is lonely."
And again he answered, "The same here."
Their five children are in the public schools.
He votes the Republican ticket and is a taxpayer.
They are known among those who know them
As honest American citizens living honest lives.
Many things that bother other people never bother them.
They have their five children and they are a couple,
A pair of birds that call to each other and satisfy.
As sure as he goes away she writes him, "The crying is
            lonely"
And he flashes back the old answer, "The same here."
It is a long time since he was a gang lineman at Cincinnati
And she was a pot rassler in a Burlington boarding house.
Yet they never get tired of each other; they are a couple.

PHIZZOG

This face you got,
This here phizzog you carry around,
You never picked it out for yourself,
        at all, at all—did you?
This here phizzog—somebody handed it
        to you—am I right?
Somebody said, "Here's yours, now go see
        what you can do with it."
Somebody slipped it to you and it was like
        a package marked:
"No goods exchanged after being taken away"—
This face you got.

THEY ASK: IS GOD, TOO, LONELY?

When God scooped up a handful of dust,
And spit on it, and molded the shape of man,
And blew a breath into it and told it to walk—
That was a great day.

And did God do this because He was lonely?
Did God say to Himself he must have company
And therefore He would make man to walk the earth
And set apart churches for speech and song with God?

These are questions.
They are scrawled in old caves.
They are painted in tall cathedrals.
There are men and women so lonely they believe
        God, too, is lonely.

EXPLANATIONS OF LOVE

There is a place where love begins and a place
where love ends.

There is a touch of two hands that foils all
dictionaries.

There is a look of eyes fierce as a big Bethlehem open hearth
furnace or a little green-fire acetylene torch.

There are single careless bywords portentous as a
big bend in the Mississippi River.

Hands, eyes, bywords—out of these love makes
battlegrounds and workshops.

There is a pair of shoes love wears and the coming
is a mystery.

There is a warning love sends and the cost of it
is never written till long afterward.

There are explanations of love in all languages
and not one found wiser than this:

There is a place where love begins and a place
where love ends—and love asks nothing.

MAYBE

Maybe he believes me, maybe not.
Maybe I can marry him, maybe not.
Maybe the wind on the prairie,
The wind on the sea, maybe,
Somebody somewhere, maybe, can tell.
I will lay my head on his shoulder
And when he asks me I will say yes,
Maybe.

FOOLISH ABOUT WINDOWS

I was foolish about windows.
The house was an old one and the windows
    were small.
I asked a carpenter to come and open the
    walls and put in bigger windows.
"The bigger the window the more it costs,"
    he said.
"The bigger the cheaper," I said.
So he tore off siding and plaster and laths
And put in a big window and bigger windows.
I was hungry for windows.

One neighbor said, "If you keep on you'll be
    able to see everything there is."
I answered, "That'll be all right, that'll be
    classy enough for me."
Another neighbor said, "Pretty soon your house
    will be all windows."
And I said, "Who would the joke be on then?"
And still another, "Those who live in glass
    houses gather no moss."
And I said, "Birds of a feather should not throw
    stones and a soft answer turneth away rats."

PEOPLE OF THE EAVES,
I WISH YOU GOOD MORNING

The wrens have trouble like us. The house of a wren will not run itself any more than the house of a man.

They chatter the same as two people in a flat where the laundry came back with the shirts of another man and the shimmy of another woman.

The shirt of a man wren and the shimmy of a woman wren are a trouble in the wren house. It is this or something else back of this chatter a spring morning.

Trouble goes so quick in the wren house. Now they are hopping wren jigs beaten off in a high wren staccato time.

People of the eaves, I wish you good morning, I wish you a thousand thanks.

SNATCH OF SLIPHORN JAZZ

Are you happy? It's the only
way to be, kid.
Yes, be happy, it's a good nice
way to be.
But not happy-happy, kid, don't
be too doubled-up doggone happy.
It's the doubled-up doggone happy-
happy people . . . bust hard . . . they
do bust hard . . . when they bust.
Be happy, kid, go to it, but not too
doggone happy.

The People, Yes
(1936)

For sixty years the pine lumber barn
had held cows, horses, hay, harness, tools, junk,
amid the prairie winds of Knox County, Illinois
and the corn crops came and went, plows and wagons,
and hands milked, hands husked and harnessed
and held the leather reins of horse teams
in dust and dog days, in late fall sleet
till the work was done that fall.
And the barn was a witness, stood and saw it all.
    "That old barn on your place, Charlie,
    was nearly falling last time I saw it,
    how is it now?"
    "I got some poles to hold it on the east side
    and the wind holds it up on the west."

.   .   .   .

    In a Colorado graveyard
        two men lie in one grave.
They shot it out in a jam over who owned
One corner lot: over a piece of real estate
They shot it out: it was a perfect duel.
Each cleansed the world of the other.
Each horizontal in an identical grave
Had his bones cleansed by the same maggots.
They sleep now as two accommodating neighbors.
They had speed and no control.
They wanted to go and didn't know where.

.   .   .   .

A father sees a son nearing manhood.
What shall he tell that son?
"Life is hard; be steel; be a rock."
And this might stand him for the storms
and serve him for humdrum and monotony
and guide him amid sudden betrayals
and tighten him for slack moments.
"Life is a soft loam; be gentle; go easy."
And this too might serve him.
Brutes have been gentled where lashes failed.
The growth of a frail flower in a path up

has sometimes shattered and split a rock.
A tough will counts. So does desire.
So does a rich soft wanting.
Without rich wanting nothing arrives.
Tell him too much money has killed men
and left them dead years before burial:
the quest of lucre beyond a few easy needs
has twisted good enough men
sometimes into dry thwarted worms.
Tell him time as a stuff can be wasted.
Tell him to be a fool every so often
and to have no shame over having been a fool
yet learning something out of every folly
hoping to repeat none of the cheap follies
thus arriving at intimate understanding
of a world numbering many fools.
Tell him to be alone often and get at himself
and above all tell himself no lies about himself
whatever the white lies and protective fronts
he may use amongst other people.
Tell him solitude is creative if he is strong
and the final decisions are made in silent rooms.
Tell him to be different from other people
if it comes natural and easy being different.
Let him have lazy days seeking his deeper motives.
Let him seek deep for where he is a born natural.
    Then he may understand Shakespeare
    and the Wright brothers, Pasteur, Pavlov,
    Michael Faraday and free imaginations
bringing changes into a world resenting change.
        He will be lonely enough
        to have time for the work
        he knows as his own.

     .   .   .   .

On the shores of Lake Michigan
high on a wooden pole, in a box,
two purple martins had a home
and taken away down to Martinique
and let loose, they flew home,
thousands of miles to be home again.
    And this has lights of wonder
    echo and pace and echo again.

The birds let out began flying
north north-by-west north
till they were back home.
How their instruments told them
of ceiling, temperature, air pressure,
how their control-boards gave them
reports of fuel, ignition, speeds,
is out of the record, out.

   Across spaces of sun and cloud,
in rain and fog, through air pockets,
wind with them, wind against them,
stopping for subsistence rations,
whirling in gust and spiral,
these people of the air,
these children of the wind,
had a sense of where to go and how,
how to go north north-by-west north,
till they came to one wooden pole,
till they were home again.

   And this has lights of wonder
   echo and pace and echo again
for other children, other people, yes.

The red ball of the sun in an evening mist
Or the slow fall of rain on planted fields
Or the pink sheath of a newborn child
Or the path of a child's mouth to a nipple
Or the snuggle of a bearcub in mother paws
Or the structural weave of the universe
Witnessed in a moving frame of winter stars—
   These hold affidavits of struggle.

.   .   .   .

The people is Everyman, everybody.
Everybody is you and me and all others.
What everybody says is what we all say.
   And what is it we all say?

Where did we get these languages?
Why is your baby-talk deep in your blood?
What is the cling of the tongue
To what it heard with its mother-milk?

They cross on the ether now.
They travel on high frequencies
Over the border-lines and barriers
Of mountain ranges and oceans.
When shall we all speak the same language?
And do we want to have all the same language?
Are we learning a few great signs and passwords?
Why should Everyman be lost for words?
The questions are put every day in every tongue:
                    "Where you from, Stranger?
                    Where were you born?
                    Got any money?
                    What do you work at?
                    Where's your passport?
                    Who are your people?"

Over the ether crash the languages.
                    And the people listen.
As on the plain of Howdeehow they listen.
                    They want to hear.
They will be told when the next war is ready.
The long wars and the short wars will come on the air,
How many got killed and how the war ended
And who got what and the price paid
And how there were tombs for the Unknown Soldier,
        The boy nobody knows the name of,
The boy whose great fame is that of the masses,
The millions of names too many to write on a tomb,
The heroes, the cannonfodder, the living targets,
The mutilated and sacred dead,
The people, yes.

Two countries with two flags
are nevertheless one land, one blood, one people—
        can this be so?
And the earth belongs to the family of man?
        can this be so?

The first world war came and its cost was laid on the people.
The second world war—the third—what will be the cost?
And will it repay the people for what they pay?

.   .   .   .

We'll see what we'll see.

Time is a great teacher.

Today me and tomorrow maybe you.

This old anvil laughs at many broken hammers.

What is bitter to stand against today may be sweet to remember
tomorrow.

Fine words butter no parsnips. Moonlight dries no mittens.

Whether the stone bumps the jug or the jug bumps the stone it
is bad for the jug.

One hand washes the other and both wash the face.

Better leave the child's nose dirty than wring it off.

We all belong to the same big family and have the same smell.

Handling honey, tar or dung some of it sticks to the fingers.

The liar comes to believe his own lies.

He who burns himself must sit on the blisters.

God alone understands fools.

The dumb mother understands the dumb child.

To work hard, to live hard, to die hard, and then to go to hell
after all would be too damned hard.

You can fool all the people part of the time and part of the people
all the time but you can't fool all of the people all of the
time.

It takes all kinds of people to make a world.

What is bred in the bone will tell.

Between the inbreds and the cross-breeds the argu-
ment goes on.

You can breed them up as easy as you can breed
them down.

"I don't know who my ancestors were," said a
mongrel, "but we've been descending for a
long time."

"My ancestors," said the Cherokee-blooded Okla-
homan, "didn't come over in the *Mayflower*
but we was there to meet the boat."

"Why," said the Denver Irish policeman as he
arrested a Pawnee Indian I.W.W. soapboxer,
"why don't you go back where you came from?"

An expert is only a damned fool a long ways from home.

You're either a thoroughbred, a scrub, or an in-between.

Speed is born with the foal—sometimes.

Always some dark horse never heard of before is coming under
   the wire a winner.
A thoroughbred always wins against a scrub, though you never
   know for sure: even thoroughbreds have their off days: new
   blood tells: the wornout thoroughbreds lose to the fast young
   scrubs.

> There is a luck of faces and bloods
> Comes to a child and touches it.
> It comes like a bird never seen.
> It goes like a bird never handled.
> There are little mothers hear the bird,
> Feel the flitting of wings never seen,
> And the touch of the givers of luck,
> The bringers of faces and bloods.

.   .   .   .

> They have yarns
> Of a skyscraper so tall they had to put hinges
> On the two top stories so to let the moon go by,
> Of one corn crop in Missouri when the roots
> Went so deep and drew off so much water
> The Mississippi riverbed that year was dry,
> Of pancakes so thin they had only one side,

Of "a fog so thick we shingled the barn and six feet out on the
   fog,"
Of Pecos Pete straddling a cyclone in Texas and riding it to the
   west coast where "it rained out under him,"
Of the man who drove a swarm of bees across the Rocky Moun-
   tains and the Desert "and didn't lose a bee,"
Of a mountain railroad curve where the engineer in his cab can
   touch the caboose and spit in the conductor's eye,
Of the boy who climbed a cornstalk growing so fast he would
   have starved to death if they hadn't shot biscuits up to him,
Of the old man's whiskers: "When the wind was with him his
   whiskers arrived a day before he did,"
Of the hen laying a square egg and cackling, "Ouch!" and of
   hens laying eggs with the dates printed on them,
Of the ship captain's shadow: it froze to the deck one cold winter
   night,
Of mutineers on that same ship put to chipping rust with rubber
   hammers,

Of the sheep counter who was fast and accurate: "I just count
    their feet and divide by four,"

Of the man so tall he must climb a ladder to shave himself,

Of the runt so teeny-weeny it takes two men and a boy to see
    him,

Of mosquitoes: one can kill a dog, two of them a man,

Of a cyclone that sucked cookstoves out of the kitchen, up the
    chimney flue, and on to the next town,

Of the same cyclone picking up wagon-tracks in Nebraska and
    dropping them over in the Dakotas,

Of the hook-and-eye snake unlocking itself into forty pieces,
    each piece two inches long, then in nine seconds flat snap-
    ping itself together again,

Of the watch swallowed by the cow—when they butchered her
    a year later the watch was running and had the correct
    time,

Of horned snakes, hoop snakes that roll themselves where they
    want to go, and rattlesnakes carrying bells instead of rattles
    on their tails,

Of the herd of cattle in California getting lost in a giant redwood
    tree that had hollowed out,

Of the man who killed a snake by putting its tail in its mouth so
    it swallowed itself,

Of railroad trains whizzing along so fast they reach the station
    before the whistle,

Of pigs so thin the farmer had to tie knots in their tails to keep
    them from crawling through the cracks in their pens,

Of Paul Bunyan's big blue ox, Babe, measuring between the
    eyes forty-two ax-handles and a plug of Star tobacco
    exactly,

Of John Henry's hammer and the curve of its swing and his
    singing of it as "a rainbow round my shoulder."

   .   .   .   .

Who made Paul Bunyan, who gave him birth as a myth, who
    joked him into life as the Master Lumberjack, who fash-
    ioned him forth as an apparition easing the hours of men
    amid axes and trees, saws and lumber? The people, the
    bookless people, they made Paul and had him alive long
    before he got into the books for those who read. He grew
    up in shanties, around the hot stoves of winter, among socks
    and mittens drying, in the smell of tobacco smoke and the
    roar of laughter mocking the outside weather. And some of

Paul came overseas in wooden bunks below decks in sailing vessels. And some of Paul is old as the hills, young as the alphabet.

The Pacific Ocean froze over in the winter of the Blue Snow and Paul Bunyan had long teams of oxen hauling regular white snow over from China. This was the winter Paul gave a party to the Seven Axmen. Paul fixed a granite floor sunk two hundred feet deep for them to dance on. Still, it tipped and tilted as the dance went on. And because the Seven Axmen refused to take off their hob-nailed boots, the sparks from the nails of their dancing feet lit up the place so that Paul didn't light the kerosene lamps. No women being on the Big Onion river at that time the Seven Axmen had to dance with each other, the one left over in each set taking Paul as a partner. The commotion of the dancing that night brought on an earthquake and the Big Onion river moved over three counties to the east.

One year when it rained from St. Patrick's Day till the Fourth of July, Paul Bunyan got disgusted because his celebration on the Fourth was spoiled. He dived into Lake Superior and swam to where a solid pillar of water was coming down. He dived under this pillar, swam up into it and climbed with powerful swimming strokes, was gone about an hour, came splashing down, and as the rain stopped, he explained, "I turned the dam thing off." This is told in the Big North Woods and on the Great Lakes, with many particulars.

Two mosquitoes lighted on one of Paul Bunyan's oxen, killed it, ate it, cleaned the bones, and sat on a grub shanty picking their teeth as Paul came along. Paul sent to Australia for two special bumblebees to kill these mosquitoes. But the bees and the mosquitoes intermarried; their children had stingers on both ends. And things kept getting worse till Paul brought a big boatload of sorghum up from Louisiana and while all the bee-mosquitoes were eating at the sweet sorghum he floated them down to the Gulf of Mexico. They got so fat that it was easy to drown them all between New Orleans and Galveston.

Paul logged on the Little Gimlet in Oregon one winter. The cook
   stove at that camp covered an acre of ground. They fastened
   the side of a hog on each snowshoe and four men used to
   skate on the griddle while the cook flipped the pancakes.
   The eating table was three miles long; elevators carried the
   cakes to the ends of the table where boys on bicycles rode
   back and forth on a path down the center of the table
   dropping the cakes where called for.

Benny, the Little Blue Ox of Paul Bunyan, grew two feet every
   time Paul looked at him, when a youngster. The barn was
   gone one morning and they found it on Benny's back; he
   grew out of it in a night. One night he kept pawing and
   bellowing for more pancakes, till there were two hundred
   men at the cook shanty stove trying to keep him fed. About
   breakfast time Benny broke loose, tore down the cook
   shanty, ate all the pancakes piled up for the loggers' break-
   fast. And after that Benny made his mistake; he ate the red
   hot stove; and that finished him. This is only one of the hot
   stove stories told in the North Woods.

.   .   .   .

          The sea has fish for every man.
      Every blade of grass has its share of dew.
          The longest day must have its end.
      Man's life? A candle in the wind, hoar-frost
             on stone.
      Nothing more certain than death and nothing
             more uncertain than the hour.
      Men live like birds together in a wood; when
             the time comes each takes his flight.
      As wave follows wave, so new men take old
             men's places.

.   .   .   .

Who was that early sodbuster in Kansas? He leaned at the gate-
   post and studied the horizon and figured what corn might
   do next year and tried to calculate why God ever made the
   grasshopper and why two days of hot winds smother the
   life out of a stand of wheat and why there was such a spread
   between what he got for grain and the price quoted in

Chicago and New York. Drove up a newcomer in a covered wagon: "What kind of folks live around here?" "Well, stranger, what kind of folks was there in the country you come from?" "Well, they was mostly a lowdown, lying, thieving, gossiping, backbiting lot of people." "Well, I guess, stranger, that's about the kind of folks you'll find around here." And the dusty gray stranger had just about blended into the dusty gray cottonwoods in a clump on the horizon when another newcomer drove up: "What kind of folks live around here?" "Well, stranger, what kind of folks was there in the country you come from?" "Well, they was mostly a decent, hardworking, lawabiding, friendly lot of people." "Well, I guess, stranger, that's about the kind of folks you'll find around here." And the second wagon moved off and blended with the dusty gray cottonwoods on the horizon while the early sodbuster leaned at his gatepost and tried to figure why two days of hot winds smother the life out of a nice stand of wheat.

> In the dry farming country they said:
> "Here you look farther and see less,
> and there are more creeks and less water,
> and more cows and less milk,
> and more horses and less grass,
> than anywhere else in the world."

White man: "I have no time to do anything."
    Indian: "Why you have all the time there
    is, haven't you?"

.   .   .   .

The mazuma, the jack, the shekels, the kale,
    The velvet, the you-know-what,
    The what-it-takes, a roll, a wad,
    Bring it home, boy.
    Bring home the bacon.
    Start on a shoestring if you have to.
    Then get your first million.
The second million is always easier than the first.
And if you get more of them round iron men than you
    can use you can always throw them at the birds:
    it's been done.

Now take some men, everything they touch turns into money:
    they know how the land lays: they can smell where the
    dollars grow.

Money withers if you don't know how to nurse it along: money
    flies away if you don't know where to put it.

The first question is, Where do we raise the money, where is the
    cash coming from?

A little horse sense helps: an idea and horse sense
    take you far: if you got a scheme ask yourself,
    Will it work?

And let me put one bug in your ear: inside information helps:
    how many fortunes came from a tip, from being on the
    ground first, from hearing a piece of news, from fast riding,
    early buying, quick selling, or plain dumb luck?

Yes, get Lady Luck with you and you're made: some fortunes
    were tumbled into and the tumblers at first said, Who would
    have believed it? and later, I knew just how to do it.

Yes, Lady Luck counts: before you're born pick the right papa
    and mama and the newsreel boys will be on the premises
    early for a shot of you with your big toe in your mouth.

Money is power: so said one.
Money is a cushion: so said another.
Money is the root of evil: so said
    still another.
Money means freedom: so runs an old
    saying.

And money is all of these—and more.
Money pays for whatever you want—if
    you have the money.
Money buys food, clothes, houses, land,
    guns, jewels, men, women, time to be
    lazy and listen to music.
Money buys everything except love,
    personality, freedom, immortality,
    silence, peace.

Therefore men fight for money.
Therefore men steal, kill, swindle,
    walk as hypocrites and whited
    sepulchers.

Therefore men speak softly carrying
    plans, poisons, weapons, each in the
    design: The words of his mouth were
    as butter but war was in his heart.
Therefore nations lay strange holds on
    each other; bombardments open, tanks
    advance, salients are seized, aviators
    walk on air; truckloads of amputated
    arms and legs are hauled away.

   Money is power, freedom, a cushion, the
    root of all evil, the sum of bless-
    ings.

   "Tell us what is money.
For we are ignorant of money, its ways and
    meanings,
Each a child in a dark storm where people
    cry for money."

Where the carcass is the buzzards gather.
Where the treasure is the heart is also.
    Money breeds money.
    Money runs the world.
Money talk is bigger than talk talk.
No ear is deaf to the song that gold sings.
Money is welcome even when it stinks.
Money is the sinew of love and of war.
Money breaks men and ruins women.
    Money is a great comfort.
    Every man has his price.
There are men who can't be bought.
There are men beyond purchase.
When you buy judges someone sells justice.
You   can   buy   anything except day and night.

.   .   .   .

The people learn, unlearn, learn,
a builder, a wrecker, a builder again,
a juggler of shifting puppets.
        In so few eyeblinks
        In transition lightning streaks,
the people project midgets into giants,
the people shrink titans into dwarfs.

Faiths blow on the winds
and become shibboleths
and deep growths
with men ready to die
for a living word on the tongue,
for a light alive in the bones,
for dreams fluttering in the wrists.

For liberty and authority they die
though one is fire and the other water
and the balances of freedom and discipline
are a moving target with changing decoys.

Revolt and terror pay a price.
Order and law have a cost.
What is this double use of fire and water?
Where are the rulers who know this riddle?
On the fingers of one hand you can number them.
How often has a governor of the people first
        learned to govern himself?

The free man willing to pay and struggle and die
        for the freedom for himself and others
Knowing how far to subject himself to discipline
        and obedience for the sake of an ordered so-
        ciety free from tyrants, exploiters and
        legalized frauds—
This free man is a rare bird and when you meet
        him take a good look at him and try
        to figure him out because
Some day when the United States of the Earth
        gets going and runs smooth and pretty there
        will be more of him than we have now.

.   .   .   .

        "Man will never write,"
they said before the alphabet came
and man at last began to write.
        "Man will never fly,"
they said before the planes and blimps
        zoomed and purred in arcs
winding their circles around the globe.

"Man will never make the United States of Europe
        nor later yet the United States of the World,
"No, you are going too far when you talk about one
        world flag for the great Family of Nations,"
        they say that now.

And man the stumbler and finder, goes on,
        man the dreamer of deep dreams,
        man the shaper and maker,
        man the answerer.
The first wheel maker saw a wheel, carried
in his head a wheel, and one day found his
hands shaping a wheel, the first wheel.
The first wagon makers saw a wagon, joined
their hands and out of air, out of what
had lived in their minds, made the first
wagon.
One by one man alone and man joined
has made things with his hands
beginning in the fog wisp of a dim imagining
resulting in a tool, a plan, a working model,
        bones joined to breath being alive
in wheels within wheels, ignition, power,
transmission, reciprocals, beyond man alone,
alive only with man joined.
                            Where to? what next?

Man the toolmaker, tooluser,
son of the burning quests
fixed with roaming forearms,
hands attached to the forearms,
fingers put on those hands,
a thumb to face any finger—
hands cunning with knives, leather, wood,
        hands for twisting, weaving, shaping—
Man the flint grinder, iron and bronze welder,
        smoothing mud into hut walls,
        smoothing reinforced concrete into
        bridges, breakwaters, office buildings—
two hands projected into vast claws, giant hammers,
        into diggers, haulers, lifters.
The clamps of the big steam shovel? man's two hands:
the motor hurling man into high air? man's two hands:

the screws of his skulled head
joining the screws of his hands,
pink convolutions transmitting to white knuckles
waves, signals, buttons, sparks—
man with hands for loving and strangling,
man with the open palm of living handshakes,
man with the closed nails of the fist of combat—
these hands of man—where to? what next?

.   .   .   .

The people will live on.
The learning and blundering people will live on.
They will be tricked and sold and again sold
And go back to the nourishing earth for rootholds,
The people so peculiar in renewal and comeback,
You can't laugh off their capacity to take it.
The mammoth rests between his cyclonic dramas.

The people so often sleepy, weary, enigmatic,
is a vast huddle with many units saying:
"I earn my living.
I make enough to get by
and it takes all my time.
If I had more time
I could do more for myself
and maybe for others.
I could read and study
and talk things over
and find out about things.
It takes time.
I wish I had the time."

The people is a tragic and comic two-face:
hero and hoodlum: phantom and gorilla twist-
ing to moan with a gargoyle mouth: "They
buy me and sell me . . . it's a game . . .
sometime I'll break loose . . ."

Once having marched
Over the margins of animal necessity,
Over the grim line of sheer subsistence
Then man came
To the deeper rituals of his bones,

To the lights lighter than any bones,
To the time for thinking things over,
To the dance, the song, the story,
Or the hours given over to dreaming,
　　　Once having so marched.

Between the finite limitations of the five senses
and the endless yearnings of man for the beyond
the people hold to the humdrum bidding of work and food
while reaching out when it comes their way
for lights beyond the prism of the five senses,
for keepsakes lasting beyond any hunger or death.
　　　This reaching is alive.
The panderers and liars have violated and smutted it.
　　　Yet this reaching is alive yet
　　　for lights and keepsakes.

　　　The people know the salt of the sea
　　　and the strength of the winds
　　　lashing the corners of the earth.
　　　The people take the earth
　　　as a tomb of rest and a cradle of hope.
　　　Who else speaks for the Family of Man?
　　　They are in tune and step
　　　with constellations of universal law.

　　　The people is a polychrome,
　　　a spectrum and a prism
　　　held in a moving monolith,
　　　a console organ of changing themes,
　　　a clavilux of color poems
　　　wherein the sea offers fog
　　　and the fog moves off in rain
　　　and the labrador sunset shortens
　　　to a nocturne of clear stars
　　　serene over the shot spray
　　　of northern lights.

　　　The steel mill sky is alive.
　　　The fire breaks white and zigzag
　　　shot on a gun-metal gloaming.
　　　Man is a long time coming.
　　　Man will yet win.
　　　Brother may yet line up with brother:

This old anvil laughs at many broken hammers.
    There are men who can't be bought.
    The fireborn are at home in fire.
    The stars make no noise.
    You can't hinder the wind from blowing.
    Time is a great teacher.
    Who can live without hope?

In the darkness with a great bundle of grief
    the people march.
In the night, and overhead a shovel of stars for
    keeps, the people march:
                        "Where to? what next?"

Complete Poems
(1950)

Bless Thee, O Lord, for the living arc of the sky over me this morning.

Bless Thee, O Lord, for the companionship of night mist far above the skyscraper peaks I saw when I woke once during the night.

Bless Thee, O Lord, for the miracle of light to my eyes and the mystery of it ever changing.

Bless Thee, O Lord, for the laws Thou hast ordained holding fast these tall oblongs of stone and steel, holding fast the planet Earth in its course and farther beyond the cycle of the Sun.

FREEDOM IS A HABIT

Freedom is a habit
and a coat worn
some born to wear it
some never to know it.
Freedom is cheap
or again as a garment
is so costly
men pay their lives
rather than not have it.
Freedom is baffling:
men having it often
know not they have it
till it is gone and
they no longer have it.
What does this mean?
Is it a riddle?
Yes, it is first of all
in the primers of riddles.
To be free is so-so:

you can and you can't:
walkers can have freedom
only by never walking
away their freedom:
runners too have freedom
unless they overrun:
eaters have often outeaten
their freedom to eat
and drinkers overdrank
their fine drinking freedom.

THE LONG SHADOW OF LINCOLN:
A LITANY

*(We can succeed only by concert. . . . The dogmas of the quiet past are
inadequate to the stormy present. The occasion is piled high with difficulty,
and we must rise with the occasion. As our case is new so we must think
anew and act anew. We must disenthrall ourselves. . . . December 1, 1862.*
The President's Message to Congress.)

Be sad, be cool, be kind,
remembering those now dreamdust
hallowed in the ruts and gullies,
solemn bones under the smooth blue sea,
faces warblown in a falling rain.

Be a brother, if so can be,
to those beyond battle fatigue
each in his own corner of earth
    or forty fathoms undersea
    beyond all boom of guns,
    beyond any bong of a great bell,
    each with a bosom and number,
    each with a pack of secrets,
each with a personal dream and doorway
and over them now the long endless winds
    with the low healing song of time,
    the hush and sleep murmur of time.

Make your wit a guard and cover.
Sing low, sing high, sing wide.

Let your laughter come free
remembering looking toward peace:
"We must disenthrall ourselves."

Be a brother, if so can be,
to those thrown forward
for taking hardwon lines,
for holding hardwon points
        and their reward so-so,
little they care to talk about,
their pay held in a mute calm,
highspot memories going unspoken,
what they did being past words,
what they took being hardwon.
        Be sad, be kind, be cool.
                Weep if you must
        And weep open and shameless
                before these altars.

There are wounds past words.
There are cripples less broken
than many who walk whole.
        There are dead youths
        with wrists of silence
        who keep a vast music
        under their shut lips,
what they did being past words,
their dreams like their deaths
beyond any smooth and easy telling,
having given till no more to give.

        There is dust alive
with dreams of The Republic,
with dreams of the Family of Man
flung wide on a shrinking globe
        with old timetables,
        old maps, old guideposts
        torn into shreds,
        shot into tatters,
        burnt in a firewind,
        lost in the shambles,
        faded in rubble and ashes.

There is dust alive.
Out of a granite tomb,
Out of a bronze sarcophagus,
Loose from the stone and copper
Steps a whitesmoke ghost
Lifting an authoritative hand
In the name of dreams worth dying for,
In the name of men whose dust breathes
        of those dreams so worth dying for,
what they did being past words,
beyond all smooth and easy telling.

Be sad, be kind, be cool,
remembering, under God, a dreamdust
hallowed in the ruts and gullies,
solemn bones under the smooth blue sea,
faces warblown in a falling rain.

Sing low, sing high, sing wide.
Make your wit a guard and cover.
Let your laughter come free
like a help and a brace of comfort.

    The earth laughs, the sun laughs
over every wise harvest of man,
over man looking toward peace
by the light of the hard old teaching:
    "We must disenthrall ourselves."

Read as the Phi Beta Kappa poem at the Mother Chapter of William and Mary College, Williamsburg, Virginia, December, 1944. Published in the Saturday Evening Post, *February, 1945.*

WHEN DEATH CAME APRIL TWELVE 1945

Can a bell ring in the heart
telling the time, telling a moment,
telling off a stillness come,
in the afternoon a stillness come
and now never come morning?

Now never again come morning,
say the tolling bells repeating it,
now on the earth in blossom days,
in earthy days and potato planting,
now to the stillness of the earth,
to the music of dust to dust
and the drop of ashes to ashes
he returns and it is the time,
the afternoon time and never come morning,
the voice never again, the face never again.

A bell rings in the heart telling it
and the bell rings again and again
remembering what the first bell told,
the going away, the great heart still—
and they will go on remembering
and they is you and you and me and me.

And there will be roses and spring blooms
flung on the moving oblong box, emblems endless
flung from nearby, from faraway earth corners,
from frontline tanks nearing Berlin
        unseen flowers of regard to The Commander,
from battle stations over the South Pacific
        silent tokens saluting The Commander.

And the whitening bones of men at sea bottoms
or huddled and mouldering men at Aachen,
        they may be murmuring,
        "Now he is one of us,"
        one answering muffled drums
in the realm and sphere of the shadow battalions.

Can a bell ring proud in the heart
        over a voice yet lingering,
        over a face past any forgetting,
        over a shadow alive and speaking,
over echoes and lights come keener, come deeper?

Can a bell ring in the heart
in time with the tall headlines,
the high fidelity transmitters,
the somber consoles rolling sorrow,

the choirs in ancient laments—chanting:
    "Dreamer, sleep deep,
    Toiler, sleep long,
    Fighter, be rested now,
    Commander, sweet good night."

NUMBER MAN

(for the ghost of Johann Sebastian Bach)

He was born to wonder about numbers.

He balanced fives against tens
and made them sleep together
and love each other.

He took sixes and sevens
and set them wrangling and fighting
over raw bones.

He woke up twos and fours
out of baby sleep
and touched them back to sleep.

He managed eights and nines,
gave them prophet beards,
marched them into mists and mountains.

He added all the numbers he knew,
multiplied them by new-found numbers
and called it a prayer of Numbers.

For each of a million cipher silences
he dug up a mate number
for a candle light in the dark.

He knew love numbers, luck numbers,
how the sea and the stars
are made and held by numbers.

BOXES AND BAGS

The bigger the box the more it holds.

Empty boxes hold the same as empty heads.

Enough small empty boxes thrown into a big empty box fill it full.

A half-empty box says, "Put more in."

A big enough box could hold the world.

Elephants need big boxes to hold a dozen elephant handkerchiefs.

Fleas fold little handkerchiefs and fix them nice and neat in flea handkerchief-boxes.

Bags lean against each other and boxes stand independent.

Boxes are square with corners unless round with circles.

Box can be piled on box till the whole works comes tumbling.

Pile box on box and the bottom box says, "If you will kindly take notice you will see it all rests on me."

Pile box on box and the top one says, "Who falls farthest if or when we fall? I ask you."

Box people go looking for boxes and bag people go looking for bags.

ARITHMETIC

Arithmetic is where numbers fly like pigeons in and out of your head.

Arithmetic tells you how many you lose or win if you know how many you had before you lost or won.

Arithmetic is seven eleven all good children go to heaven—or five six bundle of sticks.

Arithmetic is numbers you squeeze from your head to your hand to your pencil to your paper till you get the answer.

Arithmetic is where the answer is right and everything is nice and you can look out of the window and see the blue sky—or the answer is wrong and you have to start all over and try again and see how it comes out this time.

If you take a number and double it and double it again and then double it a few more times, the number gets bigger and bigger and goes higher and higher and only arithmetic can

tell you what the number is when you decide to quit
   doubling.
Arithmetic is where you have to multiply—and you carry the
   multiplication table in your head and hope you won't lose
   it.
If you have two animal crackers, one good and one bad, and
   you eat one and a striped zebra with streaks all over him
   eats the other, how many animal crackers will you have
   if somebody offers you five six seven and you say No no
   no and you say Nay nay nay and you say Nix nix nix?
If you ask your mother for one fried egg for breakfast and she
   gives you two fried eggs and you eat both of them, who
   is better in arithmetic, you or your mother?

LITTLE GIRL, BE CAREFUL WHAT YOU SAY

        Little girl, be careful what you say
        when you make talk with words, words—
        for words are made of syllables
        and syllables, child, are made of air—
        and air is so thin—air is the breath of God—
        air is finer than fire or mist,
        finer than water or moonlight,
        finer than spider-webs in the moon,
        finer than water-flowers in the morning:
            and words are strong, too,
            stronger than rocks or steel
        stronger than potatoes, corn, fish, cattle,
        and soft, too, soft as little pigeon-eggs,
        soft as the music of hummingbird wings.
            So, little girl, when you speak greetings,
        when you tell jokes, make wishes or prayers,
            be careful, be careless, be careful,
            be what you wish to be.

The Sandburg Range
(1957)

BRAINWASHING

Repeat and repeat till they say what you
are saying.
Repeat and repeat till they are helpless
before your repetitions.
Say it over and over till their brains can
hold only what you are saying.
Speak it soft, yell it and yell it, change
to a whisper, always in repeats.
Come back to it day on day, hour after hour,
till they say what you tell them to say.
To wash A B C out of a brain and replace it
with X Y Z—this is it.

SLEEP IMPRESSION

The dark blue wind
ran on the early autumn sky
in the fields of yellow moon harvest.
    I slept, I almost slept,
    I said listening:
Trees you have leaves rustling like rain
    when there is no rain.

STAR SILVER

The silver of one star
Plays cross-lights against pine green.

And the play of this silver
crosswise against the green
Is an old story . . .
              thousands of years.

And sheep raisers on the hills by night
Watching the wooly four-footed ramblers,
Watching a single silver star—
Why does the story never wear out?

And a baby slung in a feed-box
Back in a barn in a Bethlehem slum,
A baby's first cry mixing with the crunch
Of a mule's teeth on Bethlehem Christmas corn,
Baby fists softer than snowflakes of Norway,
The vagabond Mother of Christ
And the vagabond men of wisdom,
All in a barn on a winter night,
And a baby there in swaddling clothes on hay—
Why does the story never wear out?

The sheen of it all
Is a star silver and a pine green
For the heart of a child asking a story,
The red and hungry, red and hankering heart
Calling for cross-lights of silver and green.

CONSOLATION SONATA

These poplars dream,
still or shaken they dream:
they never come out of it:
to this dreaminess they are born.
        : :

        : :
Consecration is a flower,
also it is many vegetables
or again it is neither,
not a flame of rose seen
nor a new potato eaten:
        it is one tumbling moment
flowing over from a bowl
        of many earlier moments.
        : :

::

In all prisons are keepsakes:
prisoners live on memories—
their forgottens are gone—
they let the forgottens go—
out and out they sift them,
pick, choose, save these those,
leaving keepsakes to count:
this happens in all prisons.

::

::

To live big is good:
to deny much is good too.
You would have a bag of gold:
you might ask a sack of peanuts.
Be full, not so full, go hungry
Life is all time yes no yes no.

::

::

Kiss the faint bronze
of this garment of the sun.
Kiss the hem of this spun fire
brought from a smoldering,
leafed out in handspreads,
two four five handspreads.

::

::

The sun burns its gold
and this to you
is home and mother.

The night frames its stars
and this to you
is a book and prayers.

PSALM OF THE BLOODBANK

(*And hath made of one blood all nations of men for to dwell on all the face of the earth.* —THE ACTS XVII:26)

Scarlet the sunset, crimson the dawn,
    Rising moongold red curves
    through the night
    to sinking moongold red.
Poppy red a singing woman's lips.
Ruddy red the blush of true love's rose.
Fleeting the flash of a birdwing red.
    Red the cardinal's hat.
    Red the communist flag.
Token red the corpsman's right sleeve cross.
    Red the emblem cross
    of surgeon, nurse, ambulance,
    of hospital tent and ship—
    crimson blood streams poured
        together and together
        blended into one likeness,
        mingled in mute communions,
        Catholic in flow with Protestant,
        Nordic in flux with Negro.
Scoffers, sinners, deniers, in strength and rest
    from blood of Christian believers.
Help and quiet to Christian believers from blood
    of thieves, harlots, blasphemers.
           Deep, oh deep, brother,
           Deep, oh deep, sister,
              The scarlet and crimson,
              The human bloodbank red.

(*Read at the Boston Arts Festival, June 1955*)

MAN THE MOON SHOOTER

The shapes of change take their time
ai ai they take their time
moving hidden and deep
asking what the dawn asks

giving the answers evening gives
letting one tomorrow and another go by
till tomorrow comes saying,
"We are born of the yesterdays
and our unseen children wait to be born."

Where a thousand years is a clocktick,
where a hundred years is a split-second,
where a million miles is a moment of light,
the shapes go on working change
the same as forms once sea-hidden
crept to the land to become land forms,
        creeping in sun and rain,
        huddled in drizzle and fog,
        rising in mist and rainbow,
forgetful of time long or time too long,
murmuring in a music of mud and stars,
"We are born of the yesterdays
and our unseen children wait to be born.
        Take your time.
        We have all the time there is."

Where change tugs, feeds, grows,
where the-yet-to-be-born clutches and gropes
        in the folds of a womb ever weaving—
        this tells only there is to be a child,
        a shape beyond all guess and fathoming.
        Time and a womb of time tell only
        the child will have a face when it comes
        and a name given the begotten face.

        How could the Stone Age
        once born and given a name
see the Iron Age on the way to being born?
How could man carving the first wheel
        see the later labyrinths
of steel and brass wheels moving interlocked
        in a spun fabric of wheels?

How could the hairy Mesopotamian kings,
the hard-riding Persians, Jews, Greeks,
read it in the stars they were on their way out
and read too the next shapes of change to come?

Came the Romans and they did business,
likewise Moslems on horses, Vikings on ships,
barbarian strongarms riding wild horses,
saying to women or girls wanted,
hauled to the saddles by the hair,
"You belong to us by the right of capture"—
on their way to nowhere in the womb of time,
the Dark Ages given one name, Renascence another.
Magna Carta, Westphalia, Augsburg,
    names throwing shadows striped red and purple,
America, France, Russia, shaken with tramplings,
    declarations fireborn and sky-flaring,
    documents baptized and blood-dripping,
children and shapes, flags and forms—new names—
tomorrow breaking silence with fresh answers
    and the old questions hard and weather-worn:
        "Where to now? What next?"
How could Gutenberg or Caxton foretell
trucks hauling a million newspapers
roaring their banner headlines
and the desperate proverb
"Nothing is so dead as yesterday's newspaper"?

    Ever the prophets are a dime a dozen
    and man goes on a moon shooter
    forgetful of time long or time too long,
        letting tomorrow come wool-shod
        making the noise a shadow makes,
        then a name given its face.

    Machine Age given a name
went weaving into Power Age, another name—
Mass Production, Supermarkets, more names,
    Electrodynamics holding its own
till the cry "Atomic!" flashed world-wide
and "Global War" no careless bastard name,
each a child weaving in a time-hidden womb,
when it came saying, "Now I am here,"
    then having a face and a name.

The hammers of man from stone to steel,
the fire of man from pine flare to blowtorch,
the lights of man from burnt wood to flash bulb,

clew readings of man from hill bonfire to radar shadings,
the fights of man from club and sling
       to the pink mushroom of Hiroshima,
the words of men from spoken syllables
      to rushing rivers of books begetting books,
      to speech and image transmissions
      crowding the day and the night air
      for the looking and listening Family of Man—
the tools of man ever foretelling tools of new faces
          to be given new names—
            ever the prophets are a dime a dozen
            and man goes on a moon shooter.

The shapes of change
ai ai they take their time
asking what the dawn asks
giving the answers evening gives
till tomorrow moves in
saying to man the moon shooter,
"Now I am here—now read me—
      give me a name."